AT HOME WITH
HERBS

United States edition published in 1994 by Storey Communications, Inc., Schoolhouse Road, Pownal, Vermont 05261. United Kingdom edition published in 1994 by Colour Library Books, Surrey, England. Copyright © 1994, Colour Library Books Ltd.

The information in this book is true and complete to the best of our knowledge. All recommendations are made without guarantee on the part of the author or Storey Communications, Inc. The author and publisher disclaim any liability in connection with the use of this information. For additional information, please contact Storey Communications, Inc., Schoolhouse Road, Pownal, Vermont 05261.

Printed in Italy by Poligrafici Calderara
First printing, 1994

Newdick, Jane
At home with herbs: inspiring ideas for cooking, crafts, decorating, and cosmetics / Jane Newdick.
p. cm.
Brit. ed.: The complete book of herbs. 1994.
Includes bibliographical references and index.
ISBN 0-88266-886-2 : $29.95
1. Cookery (Herbs) 2. Herbs--Utilization. 3. Potpourris (Scented flower mixtures) 4. Wreaths. 5. Herbal cosmetics. I. Title.
TX819.H4N48 1994
641.6.57--dc20   94–20669
                                                          CIP

AT HOME WITH
HERBS

JANE NEWDICK

Storey Communications, Inc.
Pownal, Vermont 05261

C O N

Cooking with Herbs

PAGES 12-79

Soups
•
Salads
•
Breads and Baking
•
Cheeses, Sauces,
and Dips
•
Ice Creams and
Sorbets
•
Cakes
•
Herbal Teas and
Drinks
•
Liqueurs and Cordials
•
Gifts and Preserves

Creating with Herbs

PAGES 80-121

Sachets and Insect
Repellents
•
Pillows and
Sachets
•
Herb Essential Oils
•
Potpourri
•
Fresh and Dried
Posies
•
Balls, Trees, and
Hearts

T E N T S

Decorating with Herbs

PAGES 122-167

Wreaths and Garlands

•

Decorative Herb
Bundles

•

Garden Pots and
Containers

•

Indoor Herbs

•

Wooden Outdoor
Containers

•

Christmas Herb
Decorations

Herbs for Health and Beauty

PAGES 168-201

Bath Oils, Scrubs,
and Gels

•

Colognes and
Fragrances

•

Hands and Feet

•

Face and Skin

•

Herbs for the Hair

Herbal Information

PAGES 202-220

Harvesting and
Preserving Herbs

•

A Reference Guide
to Herbs

•

Herb Sources

•

Index

•

Credits

Introduction

The benefits of herbs are almost without limit. As well as providing delightful color and fragrance in our gardens, they offer a wealth of different flavors for cooking, and a whole variety of material for decorating our homes. Throughout the centuries, the medicinal and therapeutic qualities of herbs have helped to cure illnesses and to lift the spirit. Their spicy aromas and sweet fragrances have been used in beauty preparations and health tonics to make us look good, and feel even better.

The Ancient peoples of Egypt, China, and India cultivated herbs for their healing properties. The Chinese and Greek civilisations developed ranges of medicinal drugs based on the use of plants, cataloguing herbs for the different effects they had on the body and describing their preparation in detail. By Roman times, the culinary delights of herbs were fully appreciated, providing the basis for today's Mediterranean cuisine which combines a variety of flavors to produce distinctive and classic dishes.

In the medieval monastery gardens, herbs were grown close to the kitchen and infirmary. A variety of herbal ingredients were infused to make alcoholic tinctures and liquors, satisfying medicinal requirements and the palate, with the bonus of an inner glow.

BELOW: Herbs offer wonderful, subtle flavorings as well as pretty decorations for making sumptuous, special-occasion cakes.

Throughout Europe in the 16th and 17th centuries, mixed dried flowers and herbs were widely used in potpourris to disguise unpleasant smells. Fresh herb posies were carried in an effort to ward off disease, particularly the Plague. Linen chests were made of cedarwood or impregnated with plant oils to protect clothes from insects, and to repel mice. "Sweet" waters made from the essential oils of herb flowers, such as lavender and rose, were sprinkled liberally indoors.

In the 19th century, dried herb flowers and leaves were used in more formal decorative arrangements. At Christmas, sweet-smelling garlands and swags were draped across the fireplace, where the warmth of the fire would draw out the aromas to scent the room.

RIGHT: An original display idea, decorative herb bundles are beautiful in their fresh state, but the herbs can still be used and displayed when they have dried.

Angelica

Recently we have been rediscovering the wider delights of herbs. We use herbal teas to refresh and relax us, aromatherapy and herbal massage oils to pamper our bodies, and a broad range of herbal flavors to add interest to our food.

This book presents a selection of herb-enhanced recipes for dishes and drinks, from soups and salads to cakes and cordials. There are recipes for herbal bath and skin preparations, from cooling colognes to soothing footbaths. Potpourris and powder mixtures are included to add fragrance to every room in the house, to scent clothes and linen, and to repel moths and mice. There are decorative arrangements to craft for the home, such as wreaths and garlands, posies and trees, as well as creative ideas for displaying growing herbs.

ABOVE: *Herbal wreaths are a traditional and delightful decoration. They can be made from fresh or dried herbs – dried roses in this case – to adorn any room.*

Basil

11

Cooking with Herbs

SOUPS
Pages 14-21

SALADS
Pages 22-31

BREADS AND BAKING
Pages 32-37

CHEESES, SAUCES, AND DIPS
Pages 38-45

ICE CREAMS AND SORBETS
Pages 46-51

CAKES
Pages 52-59

HERBAL TEAS AND DRINKS
Pages 60-65

LIQUEURS AND CORDIALS
Pages 66-71

GIFTS AND PRESERVES
Pages 72-79

Soups

erbs can be the main ingredient of a soup, a subtle additional flavoring, or a finishing garnish. Their individuality can provide a new twist to classic soup recipes or provide the inspiration for new combinations of flavors and textures. Every cuisine around the world has soups based on herbs, whether they are cool and refreshing, cold summer soups or meal-in-a-bowl-type soups for winter days. Herbs are best added toward the end of the cooking time. This keeps the taste alive and unspoilt. A few hearty soups benefit, though, from long cooking with a herb, to give them a very full flavor; dried herbs may even be used for their intense taste. Freshly-chopped or snipped herbs make the prettiest garnish, sprinkled over each bowl of soup before serving. This may be an old idea, but it never fails to please the eye and the tastebuds.

RIGHT: Herbs with their highly individual fragrant flavors can be used to create a whole variety of soups for all seasons and occasions. Try introducing different herbs to your standard soup recipes for added interest.

LEFT: A scattering of freshly snipped, bright green herb leaves – in this case coriander – makes a classically inviting garnish for any seasonal soup.

Coriander

Gazpacho with Herbs

*T*his classic Spanish recipe is best made at the end of the summer when all the ingredients are plentiful and at their peak. You must use tomatoes which are really ripe and flavorful. If your tomatoes seem to taste rather bland, boost with a very little tomato paste, or replace half of the iced water with tomato juice. Serve from a punchbowl or soup tureen with some or all of the accompaniments.

3 cups very ripe tomatoes (skinned, if preferred)
2 red bell peppers, core and seeds removed
1 clove garlic, peeled
4 green onions (scallions)
1 cucumber
6 tbsps olive oil
2 tbsps red wine vinegar
1 quart iced water
Salt and pepper
4 sprigs fresh parsley
4 sprigs fresh oregano
1 sprig fresh mint

Garnishes and accompaniments:
Croûtons (1/2 inch cubes of bread) fried in virgin olive oil, ice cubes or crushed ice, chopped tomatoes, chopped cucumber, chopped onion, chopped mixed herbs, chopped hard-cooked eggs, pitted black or green olives.

Preparation and cooking time: 30 minutes. Serves 4.

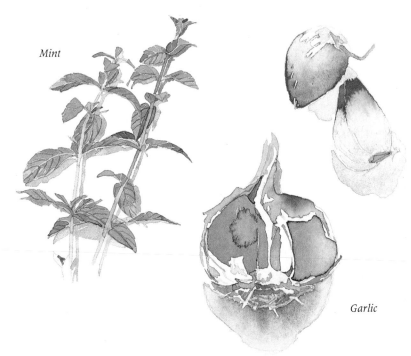

Mint

Garlic

1 Prepare and wash all vegetables and measure the other ingredients.

2 Dice all the vegetables. Tear the herbs into pieces and combine with the vegetables.

3 Blend the vegetables in a food processor until they have a soup-like consistency. Add the oil, vinegar, and enough iced water to obtain the right consistency. Season with salt and pepper. Pour into a serving bowl and chill very thoroughly. Serve the garnishes and accompaniments in small, separate bowls from which everyone can help themselves.

Sorrel and Potato Soup

*T*his is a very quick and simple recipe. It can be the basic method for other soups, such as a spinach soup, or parsley or watercress could replace the sorrel. The potato gives body and thickens this healthy and delicious soup.

1 large bunch of sorrel (about 8 ounces)
1 large potato
4 tsps butter or margarine
1 medium onion, skinned
2½ cups chicken or vegetable broth
Salt and pepper
4 tbsps chopped chives
Heavy or sour cream

Preparation and cooking time: 45 minutes. Serves 4.

Chives

1 Wash the sorrel carefully and trim the stems. Scrub the potato; there is no need to peel it. Melt the butter in a medium-sized saucepan.

Sorrel

2 Dice the potato and onion. Shred the sorrel and reserve it. Heat the butter and add the diced potato and onion. Cook over a medium heat, shaking and stirring the pot with a wooden spoon, until the onion is transparent but not browned. This will take about 8 minutes.

Sorrel

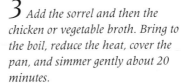

ABOVE: Sorrel resembles young spinach leaves in both appearance and flavor, and is cooked in the same ways. This sorrel and potato soup is rich and creamy – ideal for a filling appetizer to savor in the spring or fall.

3 Add the sorrel and then the chicken or vegetable broth. Bring to the boil, reduce the heat, cover the pan, and simmer gently about 20 minutes.

4 Ladle the soup into a blender or food processor and blend until smooth and creamy. Check the seasoning. Serve each portion with chopped or snipped chives and chive flowers as decoration, plus a swirl of heavy or sour cream.

Egg, Lemon, and Chervil Soup

*T*his is a light and delicate soup, elegant enough for entertaining and a very pretty pale-yellow color. Use the best ingredients and homemade broth for the best flavor. Chervil is a very subtle and delicious herb with a hint of aniseed. Serve with Melba toast, whole-wheat crackers, or crisply-toasted pita bread.

$2^1/_2$ cups chicken broth
Small bunch of chervil (about 4 ounces)
2 tbsps lemon juice
2 egg yolks
4 tbsps chopped chervil to garnish

Preparation and cooking time: 20 minutes. Serves 4.

Simmer the broth with the bunch of chervil about 10 minutes, then strain it. Combine the lemon juice with the egg yolks. Add a ladleful of soup to the egg-and-lemon mixture and return it all to the pan. Reheat, but do not let the soup boil or it will curdle. Whisk over very low heat, just until soup thickens slightly. Serve immediately, decorated with the chopped chervil leaves.

Thai Fish Soup with Coriander

*U*se a well-flavored, firm white fish for this soup, such as monkfish, red snapper, or cod, so that it will not fall apart during cooking. Eat the soup as the starter for a complete oriental meal or serve as an entrée. It is low in fat, very healthy, and tastes fragrant and fresh.

3 cups fish broth
$^1/_2$ inch fresh gingerroot, peeled and shredded
8 ounces firm-fleshed, white fish fillet
About 2 tbsps cornstarch
2 egg whites, lightly beaten
3 medium-sized zucchini
1 lime, juice squeezed, rind peeled, to garnish
1 tbsp chopped fresh coriander (cilantro) leaves
Few whole coriander (cilantro) leaves to garnish

Preparation and cooking time: 45 minutes. Serves 4.

Make the fish broth ahead of time, using fish trimmings, or a soup cube. Bring to a simmer and add the ginger. Skin the fish

fillet if necessary and cut into small cubes. Dip the cubes in the cornstarch, then in the beaten egg white. Transfer the fish to the broth, and poach about 5 minutes, or until the fish is no longer transparent and is cooked through. Do not let the liquid boil. Remove the fish and keep it warm. Slice the zucchini at an angle and cook these 8 minutes in the broth. Add the lime juice and chopped coriander (cilantro). Return the fish to the pan to warm it through. Serve decorated with whole coriander leaves and a twist of lime peel.

Coriander

BELOW: *The fragrant combination of coriander and ginger lends character to this fish-based soup. Full of different textures, it would make an interesting entrée for a special occasion.*

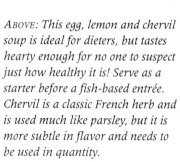

ABOVE: *This egg, lemon and chervil soup is ideal for dieters, but tastes hearty enough for no one to suspect just how healthy it is! Serve as a starter before a fish-based entrée. Chervil is a classic French herb and is used much like parsley, but it is more subtle in flavor and needs to be used in quantity.*

Salads

Salads these days are all-year-round foods, or should be. They can be a refreshing break between courses, a starter or side-dish, or a complete meal in themselves. A salad can be based around a single ingredient, or it can be a wonderful, surprising mixture of many different things. Whatever the salad, it is not complete without herbs to add flavor, zest, and color. At one time, salads often contained nothing but a mixture of many different herbs, including the leaves, buds, and flowers. We have become less adventurous these days, using herbs only sparingly, but now that we can buy fresh herbs all the year round in great variety, perhaps the herbal salad should be revived and reinstated. Needless to say, the herbs you choose should always be fresh. Dried herbs have no place here, except occasionally in certain salad dressings.

BELOW: Dare to be different and serve this melon dressed with honey, fruit juices, mint, and violet as a refreshing starter. See page 30 for the full recipe.

RIGHT: No salad is really complete without the addition of fresh herbs. Even the simplest dish of salad leaves can become delicious and decorative in this way.

Roast Pepper and Basil Salad

*F*or those who don't like the aggressive taste of raw peppers, this salad is a revelation. Broiling the peppers adds a wonderful smoky, mellow taste and the texture is soft and melting. Serve as a first course, or with another salad as a complete meal.

4 yellow bell peppers
4 red bell peppers
1 tbsp virgin olive oil
1 tbsp red wine vinegar
Bunch of basil

Preparation and cooking time: 20 minutes. Serves 4.

Basil

1 Preheat the broiler. Place the peppers whole on a broiler pan and broil under high heat. The peppers can also be broiled over a gas flame or barbecue. Turn frequently. The cooking should take about 5 minutes.

2 When the skin is wrinkled and blackened in places, quickly transfer the peppers to a large plastic bag, and fold the top over. Leave them in there to cool.

3 The skin should now peel off the peppers very easily. Slice the peppers into narrow strips, discarding the inner core, stalk, and seeds.

4 Arrange the strips prettily on a flat serving platter and sprinkle with the oil and vinegar. Strew basil leaves over the peppers, and leave to marinate for an hour or so at room temperature. Do not chill, but eat at room temperature.

Tricolor Pasta Salad

*T*his salad looks absolutely stunning with its colors of the Italian flag. It is a filling dish, suitable as a summer entrée. Serve with Italian breads and a green salad, and drink a dry red Italian or California wine with it. You could vary this recipe by using a different kind of cheese and other herbs too.

2 cups pasta spirals (or other pasta shapes)
5 sun-dried tomatoes in oil
$^1/_2$ cup black olives
$^2/_3$ cup vinaigrette dressing (made with 3 parts virgin olive oil to 1 part wine vinegar or lemon juice, plus salt, pepper, and a pinch of mustard powder)
5 stems marjoram
3 stems basil
1 cup cubed mozzarella cheese

Preparation and cooking time: 20 minutes. Serves 4.

Golden marjoram

1 Cook the pasta in plenty of boiling water until al dente, about 12 minutes. Drain the pasta, and rinse in plenty of cold water, to keep the shapes separate and stop it cooking further. Transfer to a large mixing bowl.

2 Cut the sun-dried tomatoes into small strips. Pit the olives, if liked. Mix the dressing ingredients, shaking them in a bottle, or blending them in a blender.

3 Snip or mince the marjoram and basil. Combine the cooled pasta with the cheese, olives, and tomatoes. Add enough dressing to lightly coat the pasta, then add the herbs. Stir well, and leave at room temperature, lightly covered, for about an hour, for the flavors to combine. Serve at room temperature.

Strawberry, Goat's Cheese, and Sweet Cicely Salad

Peppermint

*T*his is a wonderful combination. The touch of sweetness in the dressing harmonizes beautifully with the sharp strawberries. You could use any green leaves as the base, but the combination of curly endive (also known as chicory) and oakleaf lettuce looks particularly pretty. If goat's cheese is hard to find, ricotta makes a good substitute.

Preparation time: 10 minutes. Serves 4.

1 head chicory (curly endive) or red-leaf lettuce
1 cup strawberries
$^1/_2$ cup goat's cheese
1 tbsp chopped sweet cicely

For the dressing:
1 tsp honey
Small pinch mustard powder
1 tbsp white wine or strawberry vinegar
3 tbsps oil (olive or safflower)

Wash and dry the chicory or red-leaf lettuce. Cut the cheese into small pieces. Slice the strawberries lengthwise. Whisk the dressing ingredients together and add the sweet cicely. Pour the dressing over the salad and toss well together.

Tabbouleh Salad

Versions of this salad appear throughout the Middle East. The parsley and mint are the important ingredients and their taste should predominate; there should be about twice as much parsley and mint as cracked wheat. Though the base is wheat, the salad is light and delicious. It is refreshing and yet sustaining on a hot day. Bulgur, also known as burghul or bulghur, wheat is parboiled cracked wheat and is available from Middle Eastern food and health food stores. Flat-leaved parsley has the best flavor for this dish.

3 ripe tomatoes
1 cucumber
1 large bunch flat-leaved parsley (about 8 ounces)
1 large bunch mint (about 8 ounces)
4 tbsps olive oil
3 tbsps lemon juice
$^1/_2$ cup bulgur
5 green onions (scallions)
Salt and pepper

Preparation and soaking time: 2 $^1/_2$ hours. Serves 4-6.

1 Wash the tomatoes and cucumber, and rinse and dry the herbs. Measure out the oil and lemon juice.

Parsley

2 Put the bulgur into a large bowl, and add water to cover. Leave it to soak for two hours; when soft, drain it thoroughly, and transfer it to a serving bowl.

3 Chop the tomatoes and cucumber into small dice, and slice the green onions. Chop the mint and parsley very finely, either by hand or in a food processor. Mix the oil and lemon juice together.

4 Now simply combine everything, stirring really well to distribute the herbs. Leave in a cool place for the flavors to develop for about an hour if possible, but do not refrigerate. Season to taste before serving.

Mesclun

*T*his is a medieval French salad brought up-to-date. The choice of salad leaves is so good these days that it is easy to compose a different salad every day. A percentage of bitter leaves in a salad gives it a delicious edge and is excellent alongside all kinds of other dishes. Or use this as a salad to eat between courses.

Choose from any combination of these ingredients:
Chicory (curly endive), radicchio, rocket plant, Belgian endive, romaine lettuce, Boston lettuce, collard greens, mustard greens, escarole, watercress, endive, and lamb's lettuce (mâche or lamb's quarters).

Add herbs such as lovage, parsley, chives, chervil, tarragon, marjoram, basil, edible marigold petals, nasturtium buds and leaves.

Use a favorite dressing, spiked with a crushed clove of garlic and a little grainy mustard, crushed papaya seeds, or capers.

Marigold

Melon with Mint and Violet

*T*his is a refreshing way to eat melon, and is more like a dessert than a salad. You could also serve the melon cut into small pieces and tossed with the dressing, rather than in its skin.

2 tbsps honey
$2/3$ cup water
1 sprig mint
$2/3$ cup apple juice
1 tbsp lemon juice
1 tbsp chopped applemint
2 small honeydew or crenshaw melons
Fresh violet flowers, to decorate

Preparation time: 20 minutes. Serves 4.

Gently heat the honey in the water until dissolved. Bring to boil, add the mint sprig, and simmer about 10 minutes. Cool, and remove the mint. Combine the liquid with the apple juice and lemon juice. Add the chopped applemint. Slice each melon in half and scoop out the seeds. Pour some of the dressing into each melon. Decorate with chopped and whole violet flowers.

LEFT: *Mesclun, a medieval-inspired mixed-leaf salad. Experiment with different combinations of salad leaves, herbs and dressings to create subtle variations of texture, color, and flavor. Choose only the freshest leaves.*

Applemint

BELOW: *This delightful and unusual melon dish can be served either as an appetizer or as a dessert. Whichever you decide, it is perfect for a hot summer's day.*

Breads and Baking

*H*ome baking is fun and very rewarding. The results are always a hundred times better than anything store-bought, and the warm baking smell filling the house is one of life's great pleasures. Herbs can play their part in baking of all kinds, from rosemary-studded Italian focaccia to cheese-and-herb whole-wheat scones. If time is short, then use herbs to jazz up bought breads by wrapping them in foil like garlic bread and heating them in the oven with herb butters. Herb-flavored breads and biscuits are wonderful served alongside soups of all kinds or to accompany a salad. Adapt existing recipes that you have for favorite breads by adding fresh or dried herbs. There is little that can go wrong by doing this and you may discover all kinds of fabulous new tastes.

BELOW: The seeds of the caraway plant make an excellent flavoring for breads, cakes, and cookies. The young feathery leaves can be used in soups and salads.

RIGHT: Home-baked breads are a delicious treat made extra special by the addition of fresh or dried herbs. They are also easier and quicker to make than you might think.

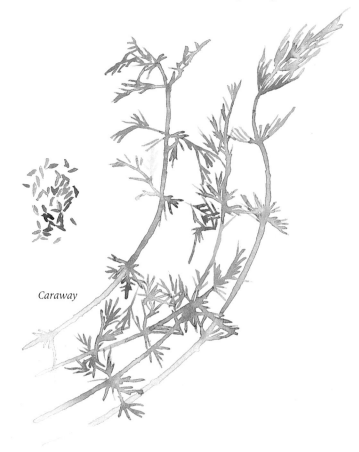

Caraway

Rosemary Focaccia

3½ cups unbleached, all-purpose flour
½ tsp salt
1 tsp active dry yeast
About 1 cup warm water
About 5 tbsps virgin olive oil
Fresh rosemary
Coarse salt

Rosemary

Preparation and baking time: 2¹/₂ hours. Serves 10-12.

1 Mix the flour, salt, and yeast in a large bowl. Add the water and about 5 tbsps olive oil. Stir with a wooden spoon, then knead with your hands. Turn the dough out onto a wooden board, and knead about 7 minutes.

2 Return the dough to the bowl, cover with a damp cloth, and leave in a warm place until doubled in bulk, about 1 hour.

3 Remove the dough from the bowl and punch it down on a floured board. Shape it into one large or two smaller circles and make dents all over surface with a wooden spoon handle. Lay the circles on greased baking sheets. Cover again and leave to rise. Preheat the oven to 425°F.

4 When the dough has been rising for the second time for about 20 minutes, brush the surface with plenty of olive oil, and sprinkle it with rosemary leaves and coarse salt. Bake 30 minutes, then reduce the heat to 350°F and bake a further 10 minutes. Transfer to a wire rack, and brush with more oil to keep the crust soft.

Chili and Garlic Tortilla Chips

*I*t is very easy to make your own crisp little tortillas and they taste even better than bought ones. Adjust the amount of chili to suit your taste. Serve them as a snack or to dip into guacamole or something similar. Your rolling-pin should be very light, a piece of sawn-off broom handle is ideal.

½ cup medium or coarse yellow cornmeal
⅔ cup all-purpose flour
Pinch of salt
1 green chili pepper, seeded and very finely chopped
1 clove garlic, peeled and crushed
1 tbsp olive oil
6 tbsps milk

Preparation and baking time: 30 minutes.
Makes about 40.

Preheat the oven to 350°F. Combine the cornmeal with the flour, salt, chili, and garlic. Now add the oil and then the milk, stirring thoroughly until you have a fairly soft dough. Knead the dough on a floured wooden board for a few minutes. Break off small pieces about the size of a walnut in its shell. Roll each of these out to a thin circle. You can cut each circle into quarters if you prefer. Arrange the circles on a greased baking sheet. Bake about 15 minutes. As the chips come out of the oven, brush each with a little more oil. Store in an airtight metal container.

Caraway Rye Bread

Caraway seeds have been used to flavor breads and cakes for centuries. Although rather out of favor now in the English-speaking world, they seem ready for a comeback. Caraway and rye are a well-tried partnership and no less delicious for that.

This bread has a chewy, moist quality from the added rolled oats. Try adding two squares unsweetened chocolate to the second-stage mixture.

For the first stage:
1 tbsp active dry yeast or 2 tsps fresh yeast
3 cups warm water
2 tbsps honey
4 tbsps molasses
1½ cups all-purpose flour
2 cups whole-wheat flour

For the second stage:
4 tbsps sunflower oil
Grated rind of one orange (no white part)
3 tsps salt
2 tbsps caraway seeds
1¼ cups rolled oats
3½ cups rye flour
2¼ cups whole-wheat flour
1 egg, beaten with 2 tbsps water, or 4 tbsps milk, to glaze
2 tbsps caraway seeds and/or raw oatmeal, for topping

Preparation and baking time: 4 hours.
Makes 2 loaves (about 30 slices)

For the first stage, mix the yeast with the warm water, honey and molasses. Add the flours and stir a few minutes. Cover and leave in a warm place for about an hour or until foaming. For the second stage, add the oil, orange rind, salt, and caraway seeds to the mixture. Stir in the oats and rye flour. Now start to add the whole-wheat flour. As the dough gets drier, turn it out of the bowl and knead in more flour, until you have a stiff but elastic dough. Knead several more minutes. Cover the dough and leave it to rise for one hour. Knead again, then cut into two, and shape into two round loaves. Glaze with egg or milk and scatter caraway and/or oats on top. Pre-heat the oven to 425°F. Leave the dough to rise again about 40 minutes. Slash the surface of the loaves and bake about one hour, or until golden-brown and sounding hollow when tapped. Cool on a wire rack.

RIGHT: Caraway and rye bread is pictured here in the background, with cheese and thyme scones in the foreground.

Cheese and Thyme Scones

*S*cones are similar to American biscuits. Use a full-flavored cheese for this recipe. These scones may not be as light as white ones, but they are delicious if split, filled with butter, and eaten warm. Fresh thyme is best, but you could use the dried herb, in which case you will need only half the amount.

2 cups whole-wheat flour
1 tsp double-acting baking powder
Pinch of mustard
Pinch of cayenne pepper
½ cup sharp cheese
4 tbsps butter
1 egg, beaten
1 tsp finely chopped fresh thyme
4-5 tbsps milk

Preparation and baking time: 45 minutes. Makes about 15.

1 Sift the flour, baking powder, mustard, and cayenne together. Preheat the oven to 400°F. Grate the cheese, reserving a quarter of it to sprinkle over the scones before baking.

2 Cut the butter into small pieces, and add to the flour mixture. Rub the butter into the flour until the mixture resembles breadcrumbs.

3 Add the beaten egg and thyme to the dough and stir in the milk with a fork. The dough should be soft but not wet. Turn it out onto a lightly-floured board and pat lightly into a flat shape about 1 inch deep. Do not overhandle it. Use a 2-inch diameter cookie cutter to cut out circles from the dough. Re-roll and cut more from the scraps.

4 Arrange the scones on the greased baking sheet and brush them with a little milk. Scatter the reserved cheese over the scones, plus a little more thyme. Bake in a hot oven about 15 to 20 minutes. Cool on a wire rack; eat while still warm.

Thyme

37

Cheeses, Sauces, and Dips

*H*erbs really come into their own when combined with the soft textures and bland flavors of most cheeses, sauces, and dips. A plain mayonnaise is transformed by the addition of plenty of chopped, fresh herbs such as tarragon, basil, watercress, or sorrel. You can also make purées of single herbs, bound with a little oil, to be added to soups, stews, and sauces of all kinds. These mixtures can be stored in small jars and refrigerated for several days. If you have time, pound the herbs in the traditional way with a pestle in a mortar, rather than using a food processor. The slower process seems to release more flavor and essential oils, as the leaves are bruised rather than chopped.

Cheeses blended with herbs are usually expensive to buy and yet they are so easy to make at home, and taste much fresher and better too, at a fraction of the cost. All kinds of soft, fresh cheeses can be used, such as cream cheese, cottage cheese, Italian ricotta, and the Mexican soft cheeses.

ABOVE: Garlic and chives make an ideal partnership as a flavoring for this creamy cheese spread, which tastes delicious with homemade breads, crackers, or biscuits. See page 43 for the recipe.

RIGHT: Label and date jars of herb purées in oil as you store them in the refrigerator, for easy identification and to ensure that you do not keep the mixtures longer than a few days.

Mustard and Dill Sauce

*T*his delicious cold sauce is the classic accompaniment to gravlax, the pickled salmon dish which has become so popular outside its native Scandinavia. The sauce goes well with all kinds of smoked or pickled fish, including barbecued and smoked salmon, and keeps well in the refrigerator for several days. Dill is a pretty, feathery-leaved annual herb with the flavor of fennel. The finished sauce is not as thick as plain mayonnaise. In this instance, tofu has been substituted for the raw egg yolk normally used.

1 tbsp tofu
2 tbsps French mustard
1 tbsp sugar
$^{2}/_{3}$ cup sunflower oil
2 tbsps white wine vinegar
Bunch of fresh dill
Salt and pepper

Preparation time: 15 minutes. Serves 4.

Parsley

1 *Such a small amount is best made in a mortar or small bowl. Measure out the ingredients. The oil must be poured into the mixture drop-by-drop, so make sure you put it into a suitable container for the purpose.*

Dill

2 *Combine the tofu, mustard, and sugar with a dash of the vinegar.*

3 *Now add the oil, drop by drop, whisking as you go. Once you have incorporated about half, you can pour in the rest in a steady stream until you have a smooth sauce. Add the rest of the vinegar and taste the mixture.*

4 *Season with salt and pepper, and add the chopped dill, mixing it in well. Taste again and adjust the seasoning and herbs if needed. Store in the refrigerator.*

RIGHT: The subtleness of dill, with its aromatic but sweet flavor, makes it a perfect partner for fish. This mustard and dill sauce is the ideal accompaniment to pickled or barbecued salmon. It goes well with whitefish and catfish.

Pesto Sauce

Pesto has become a very popular sauce these days. It is used not just with pasta or soups, but is finding its way into all kinds of dishes. Home-made versions are far-and-away better than the store-bought variety, but you will need a source of plenty of fresh basil to make it worth making. Store it for a day or so in the refrigerator, or freeze batches of it for later use. If you have the patience, make this using a pestle and mortar, but you could use a food processor instead.

40 leaves fresh basil (about 2 cups)
2 garlic cloves
Coarse salt
2 tbsps pine nuts (piñons, pignolas)
2 tbsps grated Parmesan cheese
1 cup extra-virgin olive oil
Salt and pepper (optional)

Preparation time:15 minutes. Serves 4.

Basil

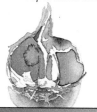

Garlic

1 Pull the leaves from the stems of the basil and tear into small pieces. Peel the garlic cloves.

2 Put the basil, garlic and pinch of coarse salt into the mortar and start to pound the leaves, pressing against the sides of the bowl.

3 Add the pine nuts, and continue to pound until they are crushed. Then add the cheese and stir well.

4 Begin to add the oil drop by drop, pounding continuously, until you have a good, creamy texture. Season, if liked, with salt and pepper.

Garlic and Chive Soft Cheese

This is reminiscent of a certain French cheese which is commercially available. It is worth blanching the garlic so that it doesn't taste too fiery. Any bland soft cheese, from full-fat cream cheese to very low fat, curd, farmer, or pot cheese can be used. It should have a fairly stiff consistency to work well.

2 cloves garlic
Pinch of salt
1 tbsp chopped parsley
1 tbsp snipped chives
1 cup fresh soft cheese
Salt and pepper

Preparation time: 20 minutes. Serves 4.

Peel the garlic and blanch in boiling water about 3 minutes. Crush the garlic with a pinch of salt. Beat the garlic and herbs into the cheese. Taste, add more salt if needed, and a little pepper. Pile into a dish and chill several hours. Serve with crackers.

Soft Cheeses Rolled in Herbs

You can use almost any rindless, soft, white cheese which is stiff enough to withstand kneading and rolling into shape, such as cream cheese, farmer, or pat cheese. Try to avoid very heavily-salted soft cheeses, or those that are too crumbly in texture. Goat's milk cheeses are particularly delicious when given this treatment, as are home-made cheeses of all kinds. Wrap some of the cheese shapes in fresh or wilted, unsprayed grape leaves and leave for several hours to absorb the flavor.

Quantities will depend on how much you wish to make. Tying the cheeses with strips of herb or lengths of chive looks very pretty too. Tuck in a fresh edible flower (unsprayed pansies or nasturtiums, for instance) as well, for a very pretty effect.

Preparation time: 15 minutes.

Tarragon

1 You will need a quantity of fresh soft cheese, and different herbs such as sweet cicely, chervil, chives, parsley, tarragon, etc.

Chives

2 Using your hands and a knife, shape the cheese into small round, flattened cakes. Prepare the herbs you have chosen by snipping them into tiny pieces or mincing them. Using a food processor would badly bruise many herbs, such as chives, however, so they are best snipped with scissors.

3 Put the herbs on a flat plate. Roll and pat the herbs onto the cheeses, then transfer to another plate, cover with cheesecloth or a kitchen towel, and chill until needed.

Ice Creams and Sorbets

The aromatic and sometimes pungent flavors of herbs are very successful when used in all kinds of frozen desserts. Herbs with a mint, lemon, orange, or rose scent are especially good, since they combine well with the sweetness and creaminess of many of these iced delights. Stronger, more savoury herb flavors make deliciously sharp and surprisingly tasty water ices and sorbets. The way to get really good herb flavors in both ice creams and sorbets is always to use fresh leaves, and to be generous with them. Most recipes require infusing the herbs in a hot or cold syrup or custard, which absorbs the flavor of the herb and becomes the basis of the sorbet or ice cream. Sometimes, additional fresh herbs are minced and added to the mixture before freezing. It is perfectly possible to make satisfactory frozen desserts by freezing them in a deep-freeze or the freezing compartment of the refrigerator, removing and stirring them as they begin to freeze, to break up the crystals, but an ice-cream maker produces the best and creamiest textures. It is also much more convenient.

Rose

FAR RIGHT: Herb-flavored ice creams and sorbets not only taste wonderful but they also look gorgeously tempting, decorated with delicately-colored herb flowers. Always use fresh herbs and in generous amounts to achieve the best flavors in these cool desserts.

46

Rose Petal Ice Cream

*T*his ice cream is indulgently delicious. The pale pink color is inviting and the taste subtle and scented. It looks particularly impressive if served in a crisp pastry shell made of cookie dough. It can also be eaten alongside soft summer fruits such as raspberries, cherries and strawberries in season with the roses. Use highly-scented rose petal varieties from a garden rose which is either deep pink or red, and make sure that you use flowers that have not been sprayed.

$1^1/_2$ cups whipping cream
$^1/_2$ cup half-and-half
4 scented roses
2 egg yolks
$^3/_4$ cup sugar
2 tsps honey
2 drops pink food coloring

Preparation and freezing time: 2 $^1/_2$ hours. Serves 4-6.

1 Put the cream, milk, and rose petals in a saucepan and bring to just below the boil. Remove from the heat, cover, and leave to infuse until cool.

2 Whisk egg yolks, sugar, and honey together in a large metal or china bowl until pale and creamy.

3 Strain the rose-flavored milk into the egg mixture and return to pan, or put the bowl over a pan of boiling water. Cook very gently until slightly thickened, but do not let it boil. Add a drop or two of coloring.

4 Chill the custard mixture, then freeze it, or process it in an ice-cream maker. Store in the freezer. Leave it to soften from frozen for about 20 minutes before serving.

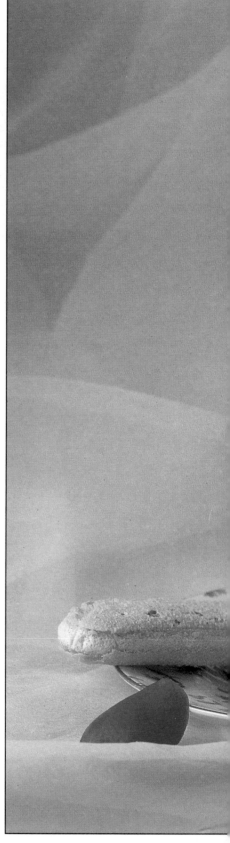

Apricot and Marigold Ice Cream

*I*n early summer, when marigolds are in flower and apricots in season, try this lovely golden-orange ice cream. Make sure you use unsprayed marigold flowers that are recommended for eating, such as the Tangerine Gem or Lemon Gem varieties. Serve with almond cookies.

4 cups fresh ripe apricots
1 vanilla pod
$^3/_4$ cup sugar
$^2/_3$ cup water
$^2/_3$ cup whipping cream
3 marigold heads

Preparation and freezing time: 2 $^1/_2$ hours. Serves 8.

Halve the apricots and pit them. Put them with the vanilla pod in a heavy-based pan with 1 tbsp water. Cover, and cook on very gentle heat. You could do this in an oven set to 300°F instead. When cooked, discard the vanilla pod. Purée the fruits, then sieve them. Dissolve the sugar in the water over medium heat in a heavy-based pan. Bring to the boil and cook 10 minutes to make a thick syrup. Pour this into the purée and leave to cool. Whip the cream and fold this into the mixture. Strip the marigold petals from the flower heads and add these to the mixture. Process in an ice-cream maker or freeze in the freezing compartment of the refrigerator.

Lemon Thyme Sorbet

*A*ll herb sorbets are generally based on a lemon-flavored sugar syrup. You can add a stiffly-beaten egg white at the stage where the sorbet is nearly frozen. If beaten then, it will whip into a snowy, light texture rather than the more grainy, icy version you get without the egg white. If you do not want to use raw egg whites, use the pasteurized dried egg whites which are available in many supermarkets.

$^1/_2$ cup sugar
2 cups water
Juice and thinly-pared rind of two lemons
4 tbsps fresh lemon thyme

Preparation and freezing time: 2 $^1/_2$ hours. Serves 4.

1 Put sugar, water, and lemon rind into a heavy-based saucepan and cook, allowing the sugar to dissolve without stirring. If crystals start to form on the sides of the pan, brush them down into the water, using a wet pastry brush. Bring to the boil, and boil briskly 5 minutes.

2 Remove the pan from the heat, and hold the base briefly under cold water to stop the cooking process. Add the thyme leaves to the syrup, and leave it to cool completely.

LEFT: *A sumptuous sundae of different herb-flavored ice creams and sorbet topped with mint and red berries. For a special occasion, decorate the glass with a trail of ivy and pin or glue on a single rose.*

Lavender Ice Cream

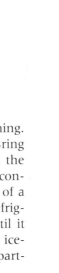

Lemon thyme

Lavender

*T*his might sound strange at first, but the subtle use of scented lavender flowers produces a delicate ice cream with an unusual flavor. It is simple to make, using a classic custard base, enriched with cream. Serve it with miniature cookies, such as tuilles, miniature macaroons, or wafers of some kind. Ensure that the flowers have not been sprayed.

4 egg yolks
$^3/_4$ cup sugar
$^2/_3$ cup half-and-half
6 fresh lavender flower heads
$^2/_3$ cup whipping or heavy cream

Preparation and freezing time: 2 $^1/_2$ hours. Serves 4.

Whisk the egg yolks and sugar together until light and foaming. Gently heat the milk in a pan with the lavender flowers. Bring to the boil, then strain into the egg yolk mixture. Return the mixture to the stove and cook over very low heat, stirring constantly until it is slightly thickened and will coat the back of a spoon. Do not let it boil. Pour the custard into a bowl, and refrigerate until it is completely cold. Whip the cream just until it forms peaks and fold it into the cold custard. Process in an ice-cream maker, or freeze in a container in the freezer compartment of the refrigerator. Serve with thin, crisp cookies.

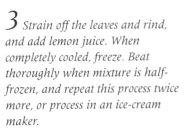

3 Strain off the leaves and rind, and add lemon juice. When completely cooled, freeze. Beat thoroughly when mixture is half-frozen, and repeat this process twice more, or process in an ice-cream maker.

RIGHT: Lavender ice cream is delicately-flavored and prettily-colored. Garnish with sprigs of lavender. In fact, all kinds of desserts can be decorated with lavender to great effect.

Cakes

If it seems odd to use herbs as an ingredient for cakes, cookies, and candies, think of the peppermint flavoring which is used so successfully in all kinds of candies, cakes, and desserts. It is often forgotten that the origin of this flavor is from a herb plant. We are very unadventurous these days in the way in which we use herbs compared with the cooks of centuries ago who combined flavors in recipes which seem to us surprisingly modern. Medieval kitchens put herbs in both sweet and savoury dishes as a matter of course. The Victorians made use of herbs to flavor sweet dishes, particularly those based around cream, milk, and eggs. A plain sponge cake or custard would be baked in a pan into which was tucked a sprig or two of sweet geranium, a bayleaf, or some lemon verbena. Just a faint hint of rosemary or lavender, for example, really enhances a simple pound cake.

Bay

Lemon verbena

RIGHT: Rediscover the culinary skills of the past and add herbs to your list of ingredients when making cakes, cookies, or candies; you will be delighted with the different flavors they create.

Sweet Geranium and Rose Layer Cake

*T*his is a spectacular layer cake for a summer party. Use any red berries to contrast well with the creamy filling and light sponge layers. Dust the surface with confectioner's sugar and decorate with clusters of frosted berries and frosted geranium leaves.

For the cake mixture:
4 eggs
$^3/_4$ cup sifted confectioner's sugar
$^3/_4$ cup all-purpose flour
2 tbsps cornstarch
$^1/_2$ tsp baking powder
5 rose-scented geranium leaves, minced

For the filling:
2 cups whipping cream
6 tbsps sifted confectioner's sugar
10 pink rose petals, finely chopped
$^1/_2$ cup berries (raspberries, blueberries, cranberries, loganberries)
Extra frosted whole berries and leaves for decoration

Preparation and baking time: 45 minutes. To serve 6-8.

Preheat the oven to 350°F. Separate the eggs and put the yolks into a large bowl with the confectioner's sugar. Whisk until light and fluffy and pale in color. In a separate bowl, whisk the egg whites until stiff, then fold them carefully into the yolk mixture. Sift the flour, cornstarch, and baking powder together and add the geranium leaves. Gently fold the flour into the egg mixture. Grease an 8 inch springform pan and line the base with nonstick baking paper. Spoon the mixture into the pan and bake in the center of the pre-heated oven about 25 minutes, or until the cake is well-risen and lightly browned. Unmold, and cool on a wire rack. When completely cold, slice the cake into three layers. To make the filling, whip the cream until stiff. Fold in half the confectioner's sugar and the rose petals. Finally fold in the berries. Spread one half of the filling over the bottom layer, lay the middle layer over it, and spread with the rest of the filling. Place the top layer on the cake and decorate it with the rest of the confectioner's sugar, sifted over the cake, and the berries and leaves. Chill until required.

RIGHT: A sweet geranium and rose layer cake makes a glamorous centerpiece for a summer celebration. Follow the method opposite to frost the red berries.

Frosted Geranium Leaves

Choose small prettily-shaped, scented geranium leaves to frost with sugar (powdered or granulated) and use as a decoration for cakes and desserts. You can also frost mint leaves and, of course, all kinds of flower petals, such as rose and violet petals.

Preparation time: 15 minutes (for 20 leaves). Serves 4.

1 Make sure the leaf is dry and leave some stalk in place. Beat an egg white with a fork until bubbly, but do not whisk it. With a fine paintbrush, paint the egg white all over the surface of the leaf, front and back, to completely cover it.

2 Quickly dip the leaf in and out of a pile of sugar on a plate, and shake it so that too much sugar does not stick to the leaf all at once. It is sometimes easier to sprinkle the sugar over the leaf from a spoon or your fingers. Make sure that the whole leaf is covered in sugar.

3 Transfer the sugared leaf to a cake cooling rack or wire mesh tray and stand this somewhere warm and dry until the leaf has hardened and turned crisp, and the sugar is completely dry.

Rose geranium

55

Applemint Angel Food Cake

*T*he applemint flavor adds a pleasant tang to this popular American cake.

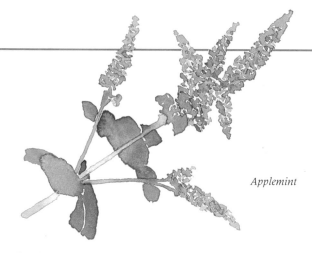

Applemint

1 cup pastry flour
2 tbsps cornstarch
5 large egg whites
²/₃ cup sugar
Grated rind of half a lime
1 tbsp finely chopped applemint

Preparation and baking time: 1 hour. Serves 6.

Preheat oven to 350°F. Line the base of an angel food pan with nonstick baking paper, but do not grease the pan. Sift the flour and cornstarch with 1 tbsp of the sugar. Whisk the egg whites until stiff, then add the rest of the sugar gradually, whisking until the mixture is very thick. Fold in the flour, grated rind, and mint. Turn into the pan and bake 35 to 40 minutes. Invert the cake, in the pan, onto a wire rack to cool, but do not unmold until cold. Serve sprinkled with confectioner's sugar. The cake should be eaten soon after baking, as it does not keep well.

BELOW: Unusually, this applemint angel food cake has been baked in a fluted brioche pan to give it an interesting shape. Decorate with herb flowers for an eye-catching effect.

Violet Meringues

These deliciously-scented meringues can be sandwiched together with whipped cream. You could add a little violet-scented liqueur, such as Strega, to the cream filling for a special occasion. Decorate the meringues with sprigs of mint, sweet geranium or, if in season, purple violas or fresh violets.

3 egg whites
¾ cup sugar
4 tbsps candied violets
Purple natural food coloring (optional)
⅔ cup whipping cream
2 tbsps powdered sugar (optional)

Preparation, baking, and cooling time: 3 hours 45 minutes.
Makes 10 meringues.

1 Line a cookie sheet with nonstick baking paper. Preheat the oven to 275°F.

2 Put egg whites into a large bowl that is free of grease. Whisk them until they form stiff peaks.

3 Whisk in the sugar, 1 tbsp at a time. Fold in the candied violets and coloring, if using. Take two tablespoons and shape the mixture into small ovals. Transfer these to the cookie sheet. Bake about 1 hour, then turn off the heat and leave to cool in the oven 1 hour. After an hour, wedge the oven door open with the handle of a wooden spoon and leave the meringues until they are completely cooled, about another hour. Remove them from the oven. Whip the cream until stiff with powdered sugar, if liked, and sandwich the meringues together using the filling.

Mint

Viola

Angelica Cake

This rich, buttery cake contains small pieces of candied angelica. You can bake it in a springform pan, a loaf pan, or even in a tube pan or bundt pan. It is excellent when eaten quite plain but you could frost it with a lemon-flavored buttercream frosting or a simple powdered-sugar-and-water frosting. If you have homemade candied angelica (page 79) then it will taste even better.

4 egg yolks
¾ cup sour cream
4 tbsps candied angelica
1 cup sugar
1¼ cups self-rising flour
¾ cup all-purpose flour
½ tsp baking soda
Pinch of salt
¾ cup softened unsalted butter
½ tsp vanilla extract

Preparation, baking, and cooling time: 1½ hours. Serves 8-10.

Angelica

1 *Line the cake pan with nonstick baking paper, if it does not have a nonstick surface; thoroughly grease the pan. Put yolks into a bowl with 2 tbsps of the sour cream and beat well. Chop or mince the angelica.*

2 *In a large mixing bowl, combine the sugar, flours, baking soda, and salt. Add the softened butter, the rest of the cream, and the vanilla extract.*

3 *Mix thoroughly, beating to incorporate air. Now gradually add the egg mixture, beating well between each addition.*

4 *Fold in the chopped angelica. Transfer the mixture to the prepared pan and bake for about 45 minutes at 350°F.*

5 *Let the cake cool in the pan 20 minutes, then unmold it onto a wire rack.*

59

Herbal Teas and Drinks

Soothing warm herb teas or refreshing summer drinks, sophisticated tisanes, and spirited wine cups all derive their taste and character from herbs. A herb tea is as simple as can be. Boiling water is poured over fresh or dried herbs and left to infuse. The strained liquid makes a soothing bedtime drink, an after-dinner digestive, or an instant pick-me-up, depending upon the herbs used. Chamomile is a good relaxant, while peppermint aids digestion, and many infusions combine healing properties with relaxing or stimulating properties, as the case may be.

Herbs can be used as a decoration for many drinks and as a flavoring to an already distinctive mixture. Imagine mint julep without the mint! In the 19th century, light wine cups were made for summer parties and outdoor events, and they invariably included herbs for flavoring and elegance. Sweet woodruff added its special scent to claret cup, and for the children and non-drinkers, ginger mint might embellish a fizzy ginger beer. Lemon balm makes a delicious addition to homemade lemonade but just a sprig will enliven the bought kind too. Flavored and scented teas are easy to make and are excellent as gifts. Always use a good, loose-leaf Indian or China tea as the basis and then experiment, adding flowers and leaves to make your own special blends.

BELOW: Herb teas vary widely in flavor, depending on the herbs used – some naturally sweet while others more bitter.

RIGHT: Herb teas have long histories as medicinal cures. They can soothe, calm, or invigorate, depending on the particular herb used.

Rose Petal Tea

*F*lower-flavored teas are quite widely available these days, but it is economical and fun to make your own. As with most China teas, these are meant to be drunk without milk, and are suitable for drinking with sweet foods, or as the perfect accompaniment to Chinese or other oriental meals.

2 tbsps scented dried rose petals (pink or red)
$1/2$ cup black China tealeaves (such as Oolong)

1 If the roses are complete dried heads, then strip off the petals and use just the largest outside ones. Measure out the tea.

2 Scatter the petals over the tealeaves and stir them together.

3 Pack the tea into suitable containers for storing or to give as gifts. Little wooden or cardboard gift boxes are ideal for the purpose.

4 To present the box of tea as a gift, add a soft ribbon bow and finish off with a single dried rose as decoration.

Make jasmine, hibiscus, or orange-blossom tea in exactly the same way. Jasmine has a strong scent, so use half the quantity you would use for rose petals, mixed into the same amount of tea. You may need to experiment and taste, until you have the proportions that you like, as dried flowers vary in their scent and flavor, depending on origin and age.

Three Herb Teas

Chamomile

Make herbal teas and tisanes just as you would make Indian or China tea. If you are making a single cup, then use a small metal infuser which you fill with a teaspoonful of the herb and put in a cup. Boiling water is poured over the infuser, which is left for a minute or so and removed when the herb tea is the right strength. Otherwise, use a small teapot kept just for herb teas and use a teaspoonful or so per person. Chamomile makes a light-golden tisane, red sage is darker and is good for sore throats and coughs, as is melissa. Jasmine tea is highly-scented and just right to drink with strong and spicy foods, or after a meal.

RIGHT: Three herb teas - the top one is a chamomile tisane, the left-hand tea is rose petal and the right-hand tea is the highly-fragrant jasmine.

Lemon Balm Lemonade

*T*his is an old-fashioned, simple lemonade, but with the extra flavor of lemon balm. The herb is easy to grow and establishes large clumps where it is happy. Although it can seed itself too prolifically around the garden, when in flower the white blooms attract clouds of bees so it is a lovely plant to have. Serve this drink well-chilled to adults and children. Some people may wish to sweeten it further.

4 unsprayed lemons
Small bunch of lemon balm
$^1/_2$ cup sugar
$^2/_3$ cup boiling water
$2^1/_2$ cups water
Lemon balm sprigs to decorate

Preparation and infusing time: 30 minutes.
Makes about 1 quart.

2 *Put the lemon rind in a small heatproof pitcher. Tear off the lemon balm leaves, and add these with the sugar. Pour the boiling water into the pitcher and stir well, crushing the balm leaves to release their flavor. Leave this mixture to infuse about 15 minutes.*

1 *Scrub the lemons well before peeling the rind thinly, avoiding as much as possible of the white part.*

Lemon balm

3 *Cut lemons in half and squeeze out the juice. Put a few fresh sprigs of lemon balm into a large glass pitcher, then strain lemon juice into it, and add the cooled, strained syrup. Top up with rest of water or half-water half-ice, and chill until needed.*

Sweet Woodruff Summer Cup

Sweet woodruff is a pretty, easy-to-grow herb whose small white, starry flowers bloom in early summer. Once picked, and as the plant dries, it releases a lovely scent similar to that of new-mown hay. It has long been used to flavor summer drinks, both alcoholic and soft.

2 tsps white sugar
1 bunch sweet woodruff (about 12 ounces)
Juice of one lemon
Juice of one orange
1 bottle chilled medium-dry white wine
2 tbsps brandy
1 tbsp Cointreau
Small bottle chilled sparkling mineral water or soda water
$^1/_2$ cup sliced strawberries
2 small strips cucumber peel

Preparation time: 30 minutes. Makes about 10 glasses.

Dissolve the sugar in a little boiling water, along with all but a few sprigs of sweet woodruff. When cool, strain it and pour into a large serving bowl. Strain the lemon and orange juices, and add to the bowl. Add wine, brandy, and Cointreau, and top up with the sparkling mineral water or soda water. Float the strawberries on top, along with the strips of cucumber peel and the reserved sprigs of woodruff. Stir well and serve immediately.

LEFT: A jug of thirst-quenching lemon balm lemonade with a glass of inviting sweet woodruff summer cup - the perfect choice of a non-alcoholic and an alcoholic drink to offer at a summer party.

Sweet woodruff

65

Liqueurs and Cordials

*H*erbs find their place in all kinds of drinks and liqueurs, no doubt originally in some health-giving or medicinal way, but these days more as a straightforward flavoring. Chartreuse, for example, is just one of the famous liqueurs made commercially which is based around the flavors of several herbs. The recipe has always been kept strictly secret. The French have long made delicious concoctions, flavoring eau-de-vie or brandy with all manner of herbs, leaves, fruits, and berries. The process is very simple to copy and the results are invariably better than many home-made wines which are time-consuming to produce and not always successful. You need vodka, gin, or brandy as a base to take the flavorings, but you can use the cheapest you can find.

Herbs can also be used to flavor syrups and cordials, to be diluted as refreshing summer drinks. Healthier and cheaper than commercial brands, they are also fun to make and what is more, you know what they contain. The best-known of these is that very English drink, elderflower cordial. English country people have always made use of the flowers and fruits of this common plant, and the results are delicious. Elderflower "champagne" is a little trickier to make and often results in broken bottles and sticky cupboards! Best to bottle the flavor in a syrup, which can then be diluted to your taste or made sparkling with soda water.

Hawthorn

RIGHT: Herb liqueurs and cordials are so simple to make and far more interesting in flavor than their commercial counterparts. Look out for attractive bottles in which to store your homemade drinks.

Citrus Herb Liqueur

There are many variations on the theme of herb-flavored liqueurs. Some are based on just one herb, others are a mixture of many herbs and other flavorings.

Leave the liqueur to mature for as long as possible, and adjust the sweetness once it is ready. Do this by adding a sugar syrup or light corn syrup until it is to your taste, or you may prefer a drier flavor and drink it as it is. The ingredients are approximate here; you may prefer to add more or omit some of the flavorings.

For a fifth of vodka you will need:
2 cloves
1 unsprayed clementine, well-washed
1 unsprayed lime, well-washed
1 unsprayed lemon, well-washed
2 vanilla pods
2 cinnamon sticks
6 cardamon pods
Bunch of fresh tarragon
1 sprig rosemary

Makes about 1 quart.

1 Stick the cloves into the clementine and put the fruit into a 3-quart wide-mouthed jar with a screw-top lid.

2 Peel the lime and lemon very thinly, ensuring that as little of the white part as possible adheres to them. Add the rinds to the jar.

3 Add the rest of the ingredients to the jar and fill it with vodka. Close tightly. Leave to mature for at least twelve weeks. Then strain, taste, and sweeten to taste.

Tarragon

69

Elderflower Cordial

Store this in clean bottles or jars, preferably sterilized ones, in the refrigerator. Dilute to taste with water, soda water, lemonade, or whatever else you choose. The muscat-flavored, lemony syrup can also be used as a sweet sauce for water ices and ice creams, in desserts, or mixed with other drinks and cocktails. Soursalt (citric acid) is available from the speciality foods section of the supermarket and from central European food stores.

2 unsprayed lemons
1 cup white sugar
2 $\frac{1}{2}$ cups water
6 elderflower heads
2 tsps soursalt (citric acid)

Makes about 1 pint.

Scrub the lemons and peel them. Cut them in half, and squeeze, and strain the lemon juice. Put the sugar and water in a pan and bring to the boil. Add the clean, washed elderflowers and simmer 10 minutes. Add the lemon rind and leave the syrup to infuse until cool. Strain the syrup, then dissolve the citric acid in the lemon juice and add to syrup. Pour into bottles and store in the refrigerator. Dilute to taste.

LEFT: *Elderflowers have a bitter, rather hot taste when eaten raw, but when infused the resultant liquid becomes grape-like in flavor.*

Elder

May Blossom Brandy

*T*his has to be made in late spring when the hawthorn is in full bloom. Pick the blossoms and shake them free of any dust and insects. Avoid washing them if at all possible. Pack the flowers into a wide-mouthed jar, and pour a bottle of cooking brandy over them. Dissolve 3 tbsps sugar in a little boiling water and add to the jar. Close the jar and shake it well. Leave in a cool, dark place for about two to three months, shaking the jar occasionally. Strain, taste, and sweeten further with sugar syrup or corn syrup if you wish.

RIGHT: *Rose brandy can be made with other types of hard liquor as the base, such as applejack. Rose brandy can be used as a flavoring for cakes, cookies, and ice cream.*

Rose

Rose Brandy

Enough scented red rose petals to fill a Mason jar
Brandy to cover them
Sugar syrup made with 1 cup water to 2 cups sugar
More fresh rose petals

Loosely pack the rose petals into the jar, and pour the brandy over them. Close the jar and leave for about one month, shaking it regularly. Simmer the syrup and add about a cupful of fresh rose petals to it. Strain the rose syrup, and add this to the brandy. Leave for another week, then strain through cheesecloth into a well-washed bottle.

You can experiment with making all kinds of other flavors of liqueur using either of the basic methods described above. Many herbs, leaves, and flowers can be tried, for example, rosemary, violet, carnation, borage, and the various varieties of mint. At one time, a drink made with young, fresh beech leaves was popular in England as a version of noyeau, the almond-flavored liqueur favored by the Victorians.

Gifts and Preserves

*H*erbal gifts are a lovely idea, combining usefulness with the giving of pleasure and fun to recipient and maker alike. Edible presents are always welcome and show special love and care in their making. A little jar of preserves or jelly is a treat to receive. These days so few people have time to do their own home canning, and yet these preserves are always so good. If your garden is overrun with herbs in the summer and early autumn, make several batches of herb jellies throughout the season. Base these on a sharp fruit, such as tart apples or gooseberries, and preserve them in small jars whose contents can be used more-or-less at one sitting. During the winter, these preserves are delicious to eat with roast meats and game or cold meats and cheese.

Flavored vinegars are another simple idea. They couldn't be easier to make, and yet presented in a pretty bottle with a special label, they are in a class of their own compared with the commercial offerings available. You can control the ingredients, so use only the best, which is what will make all the difference to the final result. Chutney-making is a wonderfully creative branch of cooking, as the quantities of ingredients are not critical and you can experiment with spices, herbs, and flavorings to create your own personal blends.

Other ideas for herbal food gifts are little bunches of bouquet garni made from dried home-grown herbs, strings of home-grown bay leaves, or wreaths made from sage or rosemary. Crackers and snacks are another area where you can customize existing recipes with the addition of particular herbs, and packaged prettily they make wonderful gifts, especially at Christmas time, when extra food items are always welcome to feed hungry guests.

RIGHT: Herb-flavored preserves, vinegars, crackers, and snacks make memorable gifts for relatives and special friends, especially when presented in attractive jars crowned with brightly-colored fabric covers and boxes tied up with decorative ribbon.

Tomato, Red Pepper, and Coriander Chutney

*T*his is a lovely, warm red-colored chutney. Allow it to mellow for a few weeks for the flavors to blend. Adjust the quantities to suit yourself, and adjust seasonings and flavorings if you want. Preserve it in small Mason jars or other small glass jars with screw-top lids. These can then be covered with a pretty circle of fabric or neat brown paper tied on with colored string.

2 cloves garlic
2 tsps mustard seed
4 cups ripe red and/or yellow tomatoes
1 large onion
4 cups sweet red peppers
1^1/$_2$ cups dark brown sugar
1^1/$_4$ cups white wine vinegar
^{1}/$_2$ tsp ground ginger
^{1}/$_2$ tsp paprika
^{1}/$_2$ tsp turmeric
1 tbsp salt
1 bunch fresh coriander (cilantro)

Preparation time: 2 hours. Makes about 2 quarts.

1 Have ready some small clean, screw-top preserving jars. You will need to cook this in a heavy-based, non-reactive saucepan. Peel the garlic cloves and mince them. Crush the mustard seeds lightly in a mortar.

Coriander

2 Plunge the tomatoes into boiling water and leave 2 minutes. Remove them and drop into cold water. Now they will peel very easily. Chop them roughly, and slice the onion.

74

LEFT: This aromatic tomato, red pepper, and coriander chutney is a sweet pickle that goes particularly well with stews and pickled meats.

Coriander

Poppyseed Cheese Straws

You can use different kinds of cheese in these light, crumbly snacks, depending on your taste, such as cheddar, Swiss, Monterey jack, and jalapeño-flavored cheeses. Whatever you choose should have a strong flavor. They should be eaten fresh, slightly warmed or reheated, as an appetizer or with a pre-dinner cocktail.

2 cups all-purpose flour
Pinch of salt
Pinch of cayenne or ground chili
7 tbsps butter
4 tbsps finely-grated cheddar or other sharp cheese
5 tbsps finely-grated parmesan cheese
2 tbsps poppyseeds
2 eggs, beaten

Preparation and baking time: 45 minutes. Makes 40-50.

Sift the flour with the salt and red pepper. Rub the butter into the flour until the mixture is crumbly. Add the cheeses to the mixture and stir well, then stir in half of the poppyseeds. Stir in just enough beaten egg to make the dough hold together firmly, reserving the rest. Preheat the oven to 400°F. Transfer the dough to a floured board and knead it lightly. Roll out by hand to cylinders about ¼ inch thick and brush with the reserved beaten egg. Sprinkle with the reserved poppyseeds. Slice into sticks about 3 inches long and transfer to a greased baking sheet. Bake the cheese straws about 8-10 minutes, or until just turning golden. Cool on a wire rack. Serve while still warm, or pack into airtight containers lined with wax paper and give as gifts.

Ginger

(cilantro) and pour it into the jars while still hot, leaving a ¼-inch space at the top. Wipe the rims of the jars, put on two-piece lids, and screw down firmly. Place the jars on a rack in a deep preserving pan half-full of boiling water, and add enough boiling water to cover the jars by 2 inches. Cover the pan, bring to a rolling boil, and boil 15 minutes, reducing the heat if necessary. Remove the jars from the boiling water and leave them to cool. When completely cold, remove the seals, label, and store the chutney.

3 Put everything except the coriander (cilantro) into the pan and bring slowly to the boil. Simmer very gently for an hour or more, until the chutney is getting thicker and jelly-like. When it is ready, add the chopped coriander

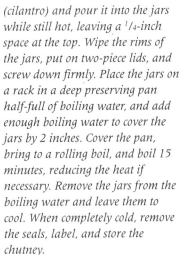

Herb Jelly

*T*his is a basic recipe which can be used as the basis for all kinds of herb jellies. You might like to try thyme, lemon thyme, lavender, rosemary, marjoram, mint, lemon balm, sage, or tarragon. Put into the smallest preserving jars you can find. This version uses lemon verbena as the basic herbal ingredient.

2$^1/_2$ pounds (5 cups) tart apples (can be windfalls)
2 cups water
Sugar
Lemon juice
1 bunch fresh herbs (about 4 ounces)
White wine vinegar (optional)

*Preparation time: 2 hours plus overnight straining.
Makes about 1 quart.*

1 Have ready some small clean preserving jars with screw-bands and metal lids. Roughly chop the apples, leaving the skin on, and including the seeds and stalks. Put into a heavy-based preserving pan and add the water. Simmer very gently until the apple has collapsed and cooked thoroughly. Ensure that it does not burn or stick to the bottom of the pan.

Lemon verbena

LEFT: *Herb jellies make wonderful accompaniments to a whole variety of meat dishes. Try teaming different herb-flavored jellies with various meats and cheeses.*

3 *To each 2¹/₂ cups juice add 2 cups sugar, the juice of one lemon, and 3 tbsps chopped fresh herbs. You can also add 1 tbsp white wine vinegar to, say, a mint or lemon thyme jelly. Put into a heavy-based pan, bring to the boil and boil rapidly until the jelly has reached setting point. Pour it into the jars while still hot, leaving a ¹/₄-inch space at the top. Wipe the rims of the jars, put on lids and screw down the bands firmly. Place the jars on a rack in a deep kettle half-full of boiling water, and add enough boiling water to cover the jars by 2 inches. Cover the kettle, bring to a rolling boil, and boil 15 minutes, reducing the heat if necessary. Remove the jars from the boiling water and leave them to cool. When completely cold, label, and store the jelly.*

2 *Strain the fruit pulp through a jellybag or double layer of cheesecloth. Do not press the pulp, or the juice will become cloudy. Leave to strain overnight or for several hours. Measure the juice.*

Sage

Herb Vinegars

Rosemary

A simple item to make but a delicious addition to anyone's pantry. The choice of herbs is yours. You can also add extras such as garlic, chili peppers, whole spices, and other flavorings to the basic herb. Certain herbs make classic vinegars. Tarragon is famous, and invaluable for making certain egg-and-butter-based sauces for fish and meat. Basil is delicious for making into dressings, and garlic vinegar has uses throughout the kitchen. Add a drop here or there to sauces, soups, casseroles, and stir-fried dishes. Try using herb flowers too, such as chives or thyme, to give a delicate color to the vinegar. Other flowers to try are primrose, violet, rose petal, carnation, elderflower, lavender, nasturtium, pansy, and edible varieties of marigold. Use a very pale white wine vinegar or a cider vinegar as the base, or for more robust flavors, use red wine vinegar.

Bring the vinegar to boiling point. Put whole sprigs or leaves of the fresh herb into sterilized, wide-mouthed bottles or jars and pour the heated vinegar them over them, leaving a $^1/_4$ inch space at the top. Wipe the rims of the preserving jars , put on the two-piece lids, and screw down firmly. When completely cold, label the bottles or jars, and leave the vinegar to steep in a cool, dark place for several weeks. Then unseal the jars, and remove the wilted herbs, which will have discolored by now. Strain the vinegar into clean, sterilized bottles. Add a few more fresh herbs for decoration if you like. The following is an approximate guide to quantities of fresh herbs to use for 2½ cups vinegar: tarragon – 2 stems; basil – 14 tbsps; garlic – 4 large cloves, crushed; bay leaf – 10 leaves; elderflower – 1 cup flowers; rose petal – 1 cup petals; lavender – ¼ cup flowers.

Candied Angelica

*T*here are several ways of candying angelica at home, but all require boiling it with green leaves to help preserve the green color. In preserving, it is important to weigh the ingredients, because it is the weight of the ingredients which determines the proportion used, not the volume. If you do not grow your own angelica, a good candy-making or cake-making supplier will have candied angelica in stock. Candied angelica is expensive, so the home-made variety would make a nice gift.

1 pound dark-green cabbage leaves or grapeleaves
1 pound angelica stems, cleaned, trimmed
and cut into 6 inch lengths
4 tbsps wine or cider vinegar
1 pound (2 cups) sugar
1 tbsp light corn syrup
1 cup powdered sugar

Preparation and soaking time:2$^{1}/_{2}$ days. Makes 1 pound.

Line a heavy-based pan with a layer of leaves. Cover with a layer of angelica stems, then add another layer of leaves, and so on, until all are used up, ending with a layer of leaves. Add the vinegar to 4 cups water and pour the mixture into the pan. Bring to the boil and simmer, uncovered, for 2 hours. Remove from the heat, and leave to cool. Discard the leaves; the angelica should now be bright green. Drain it, then transfer it to a large bowl. Add the sugar and corn syrup to a heavy-based pan with 1 cup water. Bring to the boil without stirring, then boil fairly briskly 10 minutes. Remove from the heat and pour immediately over the angelica. Stir to ensure all the stems are soaked in syrup. Cover the bowl and store in a cool place 12 hours.

Strain the syrup from the angelica and bring it to the boil again. Boil 5 minutes, then pour it over the angelica. Cover and leave another 12 hours. Finally pour the angelica, in its syrup, back into the pan and bring to the boil. Simmer 20 minutes, adding more corn syrup if it looks like drying out. Cut the angelica stems into 3-inch lengths. Dry the angelica on racks, sprinkled with powdered sugar. Store in airtight metal containers lined with wax paper.

LEFT: Be sure to tell the recipient of herb vinegars that they should store them in a cool, dark place to preserve their flavor to the maximum.

ABOVE: Tarragon vinegar is a classic herb vinegar. Try adding a clove of garlic to steep in the heated vinegar with the herb.

Angelica

Creating

with Herbs

SACHETS AND INSECT
REPELLENTS
Pages 82-87

PILLOWS AND SACHETS
Pages 88-93

HERB ESSENTIAL OILS
Pages 94-101

POTPOURRI
Pages 102-107

FRESH AND DRIED POSIES
Pages 108-113

BALLS, TREES, AND
HEARTS
Pages 114-121

Sachets and Insect Repellents

Just one of the many properties some herbs possess is their ability to repel unwanted insects. In our tidy, centrally heated, and air-conditioned homes, we are not plagued by infestations of insects in the way that people once were, but clothes' moths may still try and find a way into the closet, and at certain times of the year our cats and dogs suffer from fleas. On hot summer days, flies and mosquitos swarm indoors to irritate us, and attempt to settle on food and clean surfaces, and most country homes are occasionally visited by mice seeking shelter during the fall and winter. All these pests have had their herbal repellents in the past, and many of the ideas are well worth knowing about, apart from being another pleasant way to bring herbs into the house.

Peppermint is supposed to repel mice. The most effective way to use it for this purpose is to put a few drops of peppermint oil on cotton balls and tuck them here and there in lofts, attics, and basements, or wherever the mice appear to be getting in.

Cedarwood and sandalwood are two classic scents for keeping chests and closets fresh and free of insect pests and mice. Perhaps they are not strictly herbs because both come from the wood of full-grown trees. The small chippings are sold to fill sachets. The essential oils can be sprinkled on wooden shapes, or used to impregnate batting to put inside fabric sachets. Clean linens and fabrics, however well stored, can start to smell musty, especially if not kept totally dry, but these two scents help keep them sweet-smelling.

Cedarwood

RIGHT: Keep your clothes smelling sweet and insect-free by placing herbal sachets in your chest of drawers. Fill the sachets with cedarwood or sandalwood chippings for a woodland scent.

Lavender Bottles

*T*his is a very old idea which has been revived over the last few years. You will need fresh-cut lavender to make the bottles successfully, as dried lavender is too brittle, and the stems will not bend. The lavender will slowly dry and shrink a little. You may need to re-tie the stems together if they shrink too much. Use the bottles among stored clothes and linen.

Lavender

1 *You will need a bunch of fresh, long-stemmed lavender, about 16 to 20 pieces. The flowers should just be opening, but not too far advanced or they may drop as they dry. You will also need some strong, fine thread.*

3 *Bend back each stem individually from the thread to enclose the lavender flowers. Do this in order, working in one direction.*

2 Make a bunch of the lavender, and tie the stems tightly just where the flowers finish on the stem. Cut off the surplus thread.

4 When all the stems are bent back, tie them in place with more thread, under the bulge made by the flowers. This creates the bottle-shape. Tie the bottom of the stems with another piece of thread to hold them neatly in place. Decorate the lavender bottle, if you wish, with a pretty ribbon bow.

Southernwood

A Herb Bunch to Repel Insects

A lovely, old-fashioned way to repel moths and other insects is to make a small scented and decorative bunch to hang above a bed, inside a closet, or on the back of a door. You will need a sprig or two of southernwood (field southernwood or artemisia) which has a strange, bitter scent, several red roses, a small bunch of lavender, and one of hyssop. These can be fresh to begin with, or dried. If they are fresh, they will slowly dry out over the space of a few weeks. Make a bunch in your hand, putting the longest-stemmed plants, such as the lavender, at the back. Tie the stems together with ribbon or string.

Insect-Repellent Sachets

Make small fabric sachets from scraps or remnants of fabric to hold herb mixtures designed to keep moths away, and to scent clothes and linens. You can make purse-shaped sachets which are simply tied together or you can make small, square, flatter sachets, which are filled and then sewn closed. The fabric you choose must have a fine enough weave to prevent any of the mixture escaping. A suitable herb mixture to fill these sachets would be based around tansy and southernwood, with rosemary and lavender added. You should be able to buy all these herbs dried from a good herbalist.

The recipe gives proportions of ingredients rather than weights or volumes. This means that you can choose the measure you want, according to how much you want to make up.

Tansy

RIGHT: Tansy and southernwood are the active herbs in repelling moths. Other herbs, such as rosemary and lavender, are added to sachets for their heady fragrance.

Herb Sachet Recipe 1

4 measures tansy
4 measures southernwood
(field southernwood or artemisia)
2 measures lavender
1 measure rosemary
½ measure powdered orris root

Mix the ingredients together and use to fill sachets. Orris root powder acts as a fixative on the scents, keeping them fragrant.

Herb Sachet Recipe 2

2 measures santolina
2 measures marjoram
1 measure lavender
1 measure tansy
½ measure orris root powder

Mix all the ingredients together and use as required.

Mint

Mint is supposed to keep the flies away so it is a nice custom to hang a small bunch of fresh mint at an open window, or stand a jug of mint stems in water on a windowsill. You could try a bunch of lavender, too, for the same effect. If you do not have the fresh herb, then try dabbing a few drops of the essential oil onto some suitable material. Pennyroyal, a member of the mint family, has always been used against fleas. It may be worth trying this out by rubbing a pet's coat with the fresh leaves, or putting some of the herb in with the animal's bedding. It may just help!

Pillows and Sachets

Filling pillows or bedding with sweet-smelling, soothing herbs is an old tradition. When mattresses and beds were made from straw or other plant materials, stuffed into a linen sack of some kind, it was common to add other dried leaves and plants to keep the bedding smelling sweet and fresh. Nowadays, we might keep the spirit of this idea by putting small scented pillows among a pile of larger ones on a bed, or filling a special pillow with relaxing herbs to leave under a bed pillow to help induce sleep. As when you make smaller sachets, you should use a fabric which will keep the filling from escaping, something smooth and finely woven, unless you are simply stuffing the pillow with cotton batting impregnated with an essential oil. Silk, cotton, and linen are all natural fabrics and are the most pleasing to use.

One way of introducing fragrance into a pillow is to make a small sachet which slides into a pocket on the side of a large pillow. This is a practical method, as it means that the little sachet can be removed easily and replenished or changed when needed. Sachets and small pillows can be decorated in all kinds of ways. If you are good at embroidery, embellish your sachets and pillows with initials or motifs, flowers or hearts, or whatever takes your fancy.

The lavender bag is the most popular scented sachet and deservedly so. The fresh, astringent perfume of lavender is always welcome, so be lavish about putting these little bags amongst clothes in cupboards and drawers. Adding a fixative to the dried lavender will help to preserve the scent. At one time, sachets were always filled with a ground mixture of herbs and spices, rather than the mixed leaves and flower petals more commonly used today. These contained fixatives to hold and fix the fragrance. Sweet powder is fun to make, and you can vary the scent according to the ingredients. Experimenting with different spices, for example, can change the character of the scent dramatically from, say, warm and spicy to sharp and fresh.

Thyme

RIGHT: Herb-filled pillows, cushions or sachets are easily made and can be very decorative, trimmed with ribbon or lace, or embroidered.

Sweet Powder Mixture 1

Thyme

This recipe is measured out in volume rather than weight. Use whatever size of measure you feel you need according to the amount of mixture you wish to make. A standard cup measure is a good size to base it on. You really do need a spice- or coffee-grinder to make this successfully, though you could buy the spices ready ground and just crumble the larger leaves. Keep the grinder just for herbs and spices, if possible, or you may find the scent will flavor whatever else you grind later. Dried orange peel is very easy to make yourself. Use any peel from oranges you have eaten and dry it in a warm, dry place outdoors away from bright sunlight in the summer, or over a heat source or by the kitchen stove in the winter.

½ measure dried thyme
½ measure dried rosemary
½ measure dried sweet woodruff
1 measure cinnamon sticks
1 measure dried orange peel
½ measure cloves
½ measure coriander seeds
¼ measure star anise
¼ measure powdered orris root

2 Grind small batches of the mixture at a time, and empty the contents of the blender container into a bowl after each grinding.

1 You will need to make small bags with fairly wide-necked openings to hold the finished mixture. Strip the leaves from the stems of the thyme and other herbs.

3 Stir the finished mixture well, to distribute all the ingredients evenly. Scoop small amounts into the empty bags, and then sew or tie them closed.

ABOVE: To scent a pillow or large cushion, place a small herb-filled sachet into a pocket sewn onto the pillow, which will impregnate the pillow with its scent.

Lavender Sachets

*T*hese are particularly attractive if made in a gauzy fabric such as muslin or silk organdy. Embroider a little heart on the front of the sachet and scallop the top edges, then overstitch these. You can use plain and simple lavender flowers on their own to fill the sachets, or mix in some orris root powder and perhaps some ground, dried lemon peel in the proportions 2 measures lavender to ¼ measure each of orris root powder and lemon peel which will add a pungency to the scent.

Hop-Filled Pillow

*H*ops have been the traditional sleeping herb for centuries. Their heady scent is supposed to make you feel relaxed and drowsy, so that you slide off to sleep quickly after a tense and tiring day. You can make the pillow from any fabric you choose but when it comes to filling it, do this over some large sheets of paper, or outdoors, as the hops tend to fly around.

Hop

1 Cut out two pieces of fabric into a square, put them right sides facing, and sew them around three sides.

2 Turn them right way out and press the seams with an iron. Fill the cushion with loose, dried hops, and then close the last side with small, neat hand-stitches.

Hop

3 Finish with a ribbon wrapped once across the cushion, and decorate with a separate ribbon bow sewn onto the center of the cushion.

Sweet Powder Mixture 2

*T*his is another version of the recipe on page 90. Do not bother to grind the cedarwood shavings if they are small, but simply add them to the other ground ingredients and mix them well.

1 measure red rose petals
½ measure lavender
½ measure rosemary
½ measure dried orange peel
¼ measure allspice
¼ measure cinnamon
¼ measure sugar
¼ measure powdered orris root
1 measure cedar wood shavings

Follow the method for Sweet Powder Mixture 1.

Herb Essential Oils

The many uses of plant essential oils are only now becoming widely understood as the interest in these substances grows. Aromatherapy, the prevention and treatment of illness by massage with and inhaling of essential oils, has made these products more familiar, and many people are eager to try out their other uses for themselves. The oils are extracted from different parts of a plant, depending on the species used. Many oils come from the leaves or flowers but some come from the stems, fruits or roots, or the whole plant may be used. Herb essential oils are generally derived from the leaves of the plant in question. They are the volatile oils which hold the aroma and the important properties which may be useful medicinally or for culinary purposes. Often, these oils are used in the cosmetic industry.

There are around 300 essential oils, produced from all over the world. They are extremely concentrated liquids and should always be handled carefully. Avoid allowing them to touch your skin undiluted; they are generally diluted in a carrying oil for massage. Store them in small, dark, glass bottles to keep them away from the light, which will cause them to deteriorate, and keep them cool. Only a few drops are ever used at one time, either from an inbuilt dropper in the storage bottle or a separate pipette or eye-dropper.

Some herb essential oils can have very powerful properties. For example, thyme oil is twelve times more antiseptic than old-fashioned carbolic, and lavender oil has excellent healing properties when applied to burnt or damaged skin. A few people are sensitive to some herb oils such as thyme and cassia. Pure herb oils will vary in price according to the plant from which they derive. This is because some plants yield lots of oil, and some very little. Some oils are also easier to extract than others. If a range of oils are all the same price, this is probably because they are not pure, or have been diluted. For good results, find a source of pure essential oils.

Bergamot

RIGHT: Essential oils are widely used nowadays, especially in aromatherapy, health massages, and for making potpourri. Herb oils vary in price depending on the herb from which they are derived.

Dried Oranges

Whole oranges, or other citrus fruits, can be carved, dried, and used as decoration for a simple mixture of wood shavings. To carve the oranges you will need a special tool called a canelle knife which cuts a narrow groove into the peel. Once you have mastered its use, you can use it to cut stripes and patterns over the orange skin. You can stud the grooves with whole cloves if you wish. Keep any scraps and strips of peel and dry these to use in potpourris and spice mixtures. Once you have cut the patterns in the skin, leave the oranges in a warm, dry, well ventilated place to dry naturally. They will take several weeks to become completely dry and will shrink a little in the process. Uncut oranges will also dry, given time, but take longer than those which have been cut. Once they are dry, the oranges can be impregnated with drops of essential oil.

Wood Shaving, Chili, and Orange-Scented Mixture

If you wish to decorate this mixture with dried oranges, you will need to start preparing these well ahead of making the rest of the recipe. Natural wood shavings look best in this mixture, but dyed shavings are now available and the subtler colors can be used effectively. Other fruits can be dried for use in scented mixtures – lemons, and apple and peach slices. Choose the scent you like, but be sure it suits the style of mixture. A suitable mixture might be rosemary, orange, and coriander. Display in a container set on a low table, to enjoy its scent and looks.

1 Using a canelle knife, carve decorative designs into the peel of several oranges, not only to make them attractive, but to speed up the drying process.

RIGHT: It is best to dry more oranges than you need, since one or two might rot or go soft before drying. But the fruit must be unwaxed or organically-produced to ensure the right results.

2 Once the oranges have dried, gather together the natural wood shavings, dried chilies, an essential oil of your choice, and a shallow bowl to hold the mixture.

3 Place the wood shavings in the bowl, scatter the chilies on top, and then add the dried oranges. Put several drops of essential oil into the mixture, mixing it in thoroughly.

Scented Candles

Candle-making is not a mysterious science. It is, in fact, quite easy to do once you have the correct ingredients and equipment. The most effective candles are simple in shape and poured rather than molded. This means that you can pour the liquid wax into any suitable container which would hold a wick. Plain, thick, glass tumblers are ideal or use empty shells of all kinds. A mixture of plain, white candle wax and a small proportion of beeswax makes a candle with a nice, warm color, pale cream rather than stark white. The crucial thing to remember with making any kind of candle is that the wick must be the right thickness for the diameter of candle. If it is not, the candle may not burn properly. Candle wick is sold in long lengths and will normally have instructions stating what size candle it is meant for.

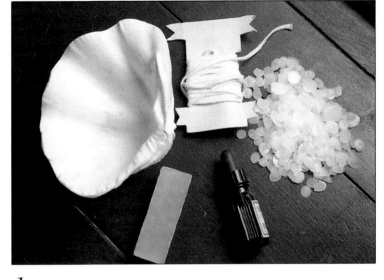

1 Choose the fragrance of oil you wish to add to the candle. It could be rose, jasmine, citrus, vanilla, bergamot (oswego or bee-balm), ylang-ylang, or citronella for outdoor candles. Candle wax comes in easy-to-melt granules these days. Make sure the shell is perfectly clean and will stand flat on a surface.

Jasmine

2 Put the wax and beeswax in a small saucepan, and allow to melt over a very low heat. Be careful if you use gas, as wax is flammable. Dip a length of wick into the melted wax and leave to cool. This will make it stiff enough to insert into the shell.

3 Attach the wick to the base of the shell with a small piece of plasticine. Support the top of the wick with a small, thin stick, such as a wooden skewer.

4 Add a few drops of essential oil to the melted wax, then pour it carefully into the shell. Leave to cool completely, then remove the stick and trim the wick to about a 1/2 inch in length.

Cedarwood Oil

Cedarwood essential oil can be used to impregnate small wooden shapes to be put inside drawers and cupboards. It is possible to buy the shapes already scented and they are often made from cedarwood themselves. Otherwise, any plywood or light wooden shapes can be used, or some of the carved and molded wooden objects designed to be used as scenters. The cedarwood fragrance can be topped up, when needed, by adding a few extra drops. Of course, you could use any fragrance you want, but cedar is traditionally used for wardrobes and other furniture designed to hold clothes and fabrics. It has a lovely spicy, woody, resinous scent.

Cedarwood

1 *Interesting leaf shapes can be easily cut from a light wood, such as balsa. Make templates from real leaves and draw around them onto the wood as a cutting guide.*

2 *To impregnate thoroughly the wooden shapes with the oil, place them in a plastic bag and sprinkle on the oil. Shake the bag and add more oil if you wish.*

ABOVE: Try impregnating wooden shapes with allspice essential oil as a more pungent alternative to the traditional cedar fragrance for scenting clothes.

Bergamot Oil

Bergamot essential oil has a fresh, citrusy floral scent, which blends well with rose geranium oil. Try combining it with a little bay essential oil, for a hint of sweet spice, and adding to a mixture of goldenberries (cape gooseberries or *Physalis peruviana*) and peach pits, garnished with nasturtium flowers.

RIGHT: *Peach pits can be used to absorb fragrant essential oils in the same way as wooden shapes, and they add an interesting texture to mixtures.*

Potpourri

Herbs of all kinds can be used to make a fabulous range of potpourris. They need not be only in shades of green, but also as bright and colorful as you choose. Think of lavender, rose, and marigold. Potpourris should be subtle in scent and as attractive as possible. These days we tend to make dry mixtures of many different ingredients, which are not necessarily scented to start with, and then add the scent we require. This is fine, but it can sometimes produce rather garish and unattractive results. Using good, natural ingredients to start with will make a better potpourri. If you grow herbs in your garden, then harvest some especially for making into potpourris and pick flowers which are suitable for drying too, to add color and different textures to the herb mix.

The basic principle for making a dry potpourri is the same, whatever ingredients you use. Mix the perfectly dry petals, leaves, seed-heads, flower-heads, and whatever you have chosen with ground or whole spices, other scented ingredients such as citrus peels, and the all-important fixatives which will help the potpourri to retain its scent. Then drops of essential oil are added to boost the perfume. This is where you can be quite creative, and make your own special fragrances to suit your house and your taste. The most widely used fixative is powdered orris root which is made from the rhizome of an iris. The powder looks like ground ginger, and has a very faint perfume of violets. It has the ability, though, to "fix" other scents and make them last longer. You may prefer simply to use an essential oil and keep topping it up when the fragrance fades. Orris root powder is available from herbalists.

Lime blossom

RIGHT: *Once you have tried some of these recipes, experiment with your own combinations of different dried materials and scents, perhaps for different rooms in your home, or for special occasions or gifts.*

Some of the herbs suitable for potpourris are thyme, rosemary, bay, sage, lemon verbena, scented geranium (*Pelargonium odoratissimum*), chamomile, lime (linden) blossom, savory, hyssop, marigold, rose, lavender, and pineapple sage. It is possible to buy essential oils of many of these herbs, and it is best to use the right oil for the herb you are using for a potpourri, but you may like to combine herbs, or add citrus oils or spice oils, too.

The amounts have been given in volume, based on a standard measuring cup. You can increase or decrease the amounts to suit yourself.

Mixed Leaf and Herb Potpourri

*T*his makes a pretty, soft-green mixture which looks best displayed in a rustic pottery bowl or a textured basket. The leaves you choose are not crucial, just try to get a good mix of large and small types.

1 cup dried eucalyptus leaves
1 cup dried bay leaves
1 cup lemon verbena leaves
½ cup uva-ursi (bearberry) leaves
½ cup dried thyme/rosemary/sage etc.
A few whole sprigs dried thyme
½ cup powdered orris root
Several drops of lime (linden) flower, vervain,
or rosemary essential oil

1 Put all the leaves into a large mixing bowl.

Eucalyptus

Red Rose Potpourri

A very simple mixture again, but one which always pleases. Using whole rosebuds makes a much more interesting mixture than petals. You can buy bags of loose rose heads or buy the more expensive dried roses on stems and pick them off.

5 cups red or pink whole rosebuds
½ cup powdered orris root
¼ cup ground cloves
¼ cup ground allspice
4 drops oil of rose geranium
4 drops oil of ylang-ylang

Put the rosebuds into a large bowl, and add the orris root and ground spices. Mix these very well together. Add the oils, drop by drop, stirring the mixture all the time. Scoop it into paper bags and fold over the tops. Leave the bags in a cool dark place for at least four weeks to cure, before displaying the potpourri in small bowls or boxes.

2 Add the orris root, and mix really well with your hands or a wooden spoon.

ABOVE: While keeping the overall subtle green color scheme of this lovely potpourri, use a range of variegated leaves to add interesting highlights.

3 Add several drops of the oils, stirring as you do so. Put the mixture into large paper bags, fold them over and secure them loosely with a large clip or clothespin. Leave in a cool, dark place to cure, preferably for several weeks, before displaying.

Marigold Potpourri

*T*his is a lovely bright and sparkling potpourri with the fresh and fruity scent of oranges, and a hint of spice. Some whole spices, flower heads, and slices of dried orange add greatly to the finished look of this potpourri. Marigolds are simple to grow, and they dry very easily, retaining their strong orange color. The kind you need are pot marigolds (*Calendula officinalis*); other varieties have an acrid smell which some people find unpleasant.

4 cups dried marigold petals (or a mixture of
yellow-and-orange flower petals, e.g. chamomile)
1 cup whole marigold flower heads
1 cup dried orange peel
½ cup small sticks of cinnamon
½ cup powdered orris root
¼ cup frankincense crystals
¼ cup ground cloves
¼ cup ground nutmeg
3 drops oil of bitter (sour) orange
3 drops oil of lemon
3 drops oil of cinnamon
Whole rings of dried orange to decorate

1 Put the dried flower heads and petals into a large bowl.

Marigold

2 Add the peel, cinnamon, orris root, the frankincense (another fixative), and ground spices, and stir very thoroughly.

3 Add the essential oils, drop by drop, stirring the mixture as you do so. Put the mixture into paper bags, fold the tops over and secure lightly. Leave in a cool, dark place for at least four weeks to cure, before displaying. Add the dried orange rings to the dish.

106

Lavender Potpourri

*T*his is often made from nothing more than plain lavender, but adding the fixative and oils will make it last longer. You can also add a little more color by using some blue flower heads; the type of flower will vary according to where you live. Decorate the finished bowl with a little bundle of lavender flower stems, tied with string or thread, or more elaborately tied with ribbon. Display this potpourri in a wide, shallow bowl and make it in a fairly large quantity for the best effect. Dried lavender sold loose is usually not the dark, purple-flowered varieties but if you grow your own lavender the color choice is yours, depending upon which varieties you grow.

5 cups dried lavender
1 cup blue flower heads or petals (optional)
½ cup powdered orris root
10 drops oil of lavender

Put the dried flowers into a large bowl. Add the orris root powder and mix very well. Add the oil, drop by drop, stirring the mixture as you do so. Scoop the potpourri into paper bags, turn over the tops, and leave in a cool dark place to cure for about four weeks before displaying.

Fresh and Dried Posies

For as long as people have grown herbs and flowers, they have picked small bunches of them and made them into little posies in the hand. Posies make charming gifts and are the simplest and prettiest of any kind of flower arrangement. They also look pretty hanging from a ribbon to decorate a door or an item of furniture. All through the year, those with yards can usually find enough herbs and flowers to pick and make a tiny, scented posy. Centuries ago, these little flower bunches had a more serious purpose than just to amuse or delight. "Tussie-mussies", as they were called, were carried by the "Great and the Good" in an attempt to keep illness and infection at bay. Until the last century, judges and other dignitaries in England and Scotland carried a tussie-mussie with them, in the mistaken belief that smelling one would fend off disease. In those days, it was thought that a bad smell from drains or the street carried the illnesses, and that a sweet scent would counteract this. The tradition lingers on to this day in the Maundy Thursday ceremony, on the day before Good Friday, when the British monarch carries a posy while distributing specially minted coins to the poor, a ritual that dates back well into the Middle Ages.

As well as fresh herb posies, it is possible to make dried ones too, using a mixture of scented and non-scented materials. Any posy looks best if it is carefully thought out, with a good balance of colors and flower shapes, and perhaps a ring of leaves used as edging. Gray-leaved herbs look very pretty mixed in with other plants, as they dry to a soft silver color. Examples are southernwood (field southernwood or artemisia), silver thyme, sage, and lavender. Once you have bunched up the herbs and flowers into the right size of posy, tie the stems with string or fine wire, and cut the base of the stems to a uniform length. Dried posies can have a little paper or lace collar, made from a doily, added to them for a "Victorian" look.

Hyssop

RIGHT: To create longer-lasting displays of fresh posies, place them in small glass vases – even attractively-shaped or decorated wine glasses – topped up with water.

108

To make the best dried posy, you should use ingredients which have already been dried, but you can also experiment with making small, fresh posies which are then dried complete. Remember that these will shrink quite a bit as they dry and some of the herbs and flowers may dry at different rates. The effect will be very different from a posy made the first way, but the results are sometimes very pretty and unusual.

Bergamot

Fresh Herb Posy

A fresh herb posy made slightly larger than a tussie-mussie makes a very pretty flower arrangement to stand in a pitcher or any suitable container. This version has a red rose as the focal point, and a lovely combination of other flowering herbs, including hyssop, applemint, pink bergamot (oswego or bee-balm), and the starry, blue flowers of borage. Begin with a single bloom, then build up the posy, adding rings of a different variety of flower around the central bloom. Here, the posy is edged with flowering hyssop. You can also make simpler versions, using just one type of flower, such as the nasturtium posy.

BELOW: Traditionally, the outer ring of a posy or "tussie-mussie" consists of a fragrant herb, so that the scent is released by the warmth of the hand that carries it. This posy is edged with minty hyssop.

Kitchen Herb Posies

*I*f you grow plenty of herbs in the garden, then some of the surplus can be dried for using in the winter. Even if you don't use all the leaves in cooking, the bunches are pretty simply hanging as decorations. Always harvest herbs when they are dry, and do so just before the middle of the day, when their volatile oils – and therefore their scent – is at its strongest. Make small bunches and tie them tightly with wire. Make hooks from a length of thickish

wire and hang the bunches by these hooks in a warm airy place. The ideal location is near a kitchen stove or the basement furnace in winter, but a well-ventilated and shaded place outdoors in the summer will do. Depending on the climatic conditions, the bunches will take from five to ten days to dry completely. Suitable herbs for this air-drying include rosemary, thyme, sage, hyssop, savory, southernwood, and marjoram.

Bouquet Garni Bunches

Traditional bouquet garni bunches make all the difference in flavor to soups, sauces, and casseroles. Rather out of favor these days, they are nevertheless easy to put together if you have a fairly well-stocked herb garden. The classic bouquet garni contains a sprig of thyme, bay leaf, curly-leaved parsley, and sometimes a small piece of celery stalk. You can adapt the herbs depending on the dish they are to flavor. Leave plenty of stalk on the parsley, as this is where all its flavor lies. You can also make bouquets garnis from dried herbs, but try to use fresh parsley.

To make a collection of herb bouquets as a gift, gather fresh herbs together and once they are made up, keep them fresh in a shallow basket by covering the stem bases with plastic wrap or tucking them into damp moss. Freeze some for winter, packing them in plastic wrap and then heavy-duty aluminum foil.

2 Combine a bayleaf or two with a sprig of thyme and parsley, for a classic combination. Tie with string.

1 Sort the various herbs, and cut them into small manageable pieces. Cut some short lengths of string to have ready.

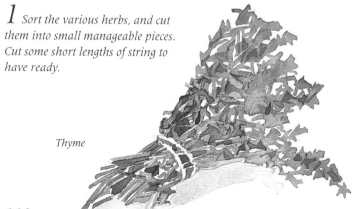

Thyme

3 If the bunches are to be gifts, label them with a suggestion about how to use them. This version is for a casserole, or for laying beneath a roast of lamb. For pork, substitute sage for the thyme, and push the mixture through a dried apple ring before tying. For beef, use the same combination as for lamb, but add a sprig of chervil and one of coriander (cilantro).

Yellow Rose and Cinnamon Posy

*T*he finished posy is very pretty and sweet-smelling. Drops of essential oil, either lavender or cinnamon, can also be added, which will boost the fragrance further.

12 dried yellow roses
12 cinnamon sticks
12 safflowers
12 echinops flowers (or other thistles)
24 stems of lavender

Sort the various ingredients into separate piles. Start by putting one of each ingredient together into a bunch. Continue to do this, using twice as much lavender throughout the bunch. When you have a tidy bunch and have used up all the flowers, tie the stems together tightly with wire and trim them off at the base.

Balls, Trees, and Hearts

The decorative possibilities of dried herbs are really very great. They can be used in the same ways as dried flowers, and, in fact, many herbs also fall into the dried-flower category. Think of roses or lavender, for example. The advantage of many herbs is that they have their own natural fragrances which remain quite strong when dry. You can sprinkle a few drops of an essential oil over any of these decorations to add fragrance. They will soak it up and release it gently, particularly when slightly warmed, near a lamp, for example.

Many of these more complicated decorations are very much more easily made using a hot-melt glue-gun rather than conventional glues and adhesives. Because glue from the gun sets firmly in such a short time, it speeds up jobs which would otherwise be very tedious, such as gluing individual leaves onto a preformed foam shape. The simplest glue-guns are inexpensive. If you do not use one, then find an adhesive which holds and glues as quickly as possible, and is suitable for use with natural materials.

Floral foam is suitable for cutting into various shapes with a craft knife and using as a base for herbal creations. The brown type sold for dried flowers is fine, but it is more expensive than the green sort sold for fresh flowers. The green is softer and easier to cut into shape, and it will be invisible if you completely cover it with plant materials. Use whichever you prefer to work with, or can get hold of most easily.

Certain flowers, such as roses, are often sold stemless and loose in bags. These are less expensive than the dried roses complete with stems which, in any case, are a waste for these kinds of decorations. It is worth spending some time on the preparation of the materials for the decorations before you start assembling them. Pick out a batch of matching flowers or leaves first and discard the rest in order to achieve the neatest and most symmetrical end results.

Marjoram

RIGHT: *You can buy floral foam in a range of shapes nowadays, to use as bases for herb decorations. However, it is easy to cut your own shapes from foam block or board.*

Bay Leaf Tree

*T*his is a variation on the more usual round or conical topiary tree. It uses dried bay leaves to cover a tall, rectangular foam shape. An old porous clay plant-pot is a sympathetic container, but you could use something else if you wish. You will need:

Piece of floral foam
10 straight twigs
About 100 bay leaves
1 porous clay plant-pot
Reindeer moss to cover the foam in the pot
Wire
Dried orange slices
Ribbon

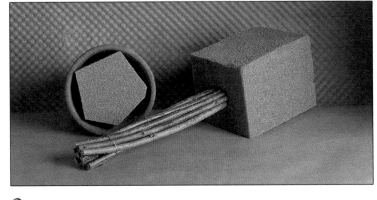

2 Push the twigs into the foam rectangle. Fill the pot with foam, too, and push the twig stems down into this securely.

1 Cut the foam into a tall rectangle. Bind the twigs together into a bundle, and wire them tightly at each end. Sort the bay leaves into piles of equal-sized leaves.

3 Start to glue the leaves neatly in place, snipping off any overlapping edges.

4 Completely cover the foam with leaves. Cover the foam in the pot with pieces of reindeer moss. Wire 2 slices of dried orange together, and attach them to a ribbon bow with wire. Push this wire into the foam in the pot.

Pink Rose Heart

Rose

You will need a length of moss ribbon, which is available from craft stores or florists specializing in dried arrangements, and dried pink roses. Alternatively, make a heart from wire by pinching halfway along a piece (see step 1), then bending back the ends to meet. Form a loop in one end and a hook in the other and attach. Bind moss onto the heart using fine reel wire.

Red Rose Ball

*T*his is very simple to make. You will need a foam sphere, of whatever size you choose, and plenty of rose-heads. You will find that it takes a very large number of roses to cover the sphere. Glue them in place, working in a line around the circumference to begin with, then working in rows toward the top, and finally work downward in the same way. Hold the ball gently as you glue, so as not to crush the flower heads. It may be easier to spear the ball onto a wooden skewer while you work. Tie a cord or ribbon around the finished sphere if you wish to hang it on a door or a wall.

1 Cut the moss ribbon to the length required to make a heart-shape. Pinch it halfway along the length, and dab it with a little glue. Bend the ribbon backward onto itself until it is firmly glued.

2 Now bend the two ends back the other way, to make a point at the bottom. Glue the two ends together. You will find that a heart-shape forms naturally.

3 Glue the roses right around the heart, on the top edge of the ribbon. Attach a cord or ribbon, if you wish to hang the finished heart.

ABOVE: *As a contrast in texture, color, and fragrance to these rose balls, you could coat small foam balls with glue and then roll them in dried lavender flowers.*

Marjoram and Poppy Basket

*T*his idea relies on the heart-shaped container for its special effect but it would look equally pretty if made into a round or square basket. Again, the glue-gun is necessary to fix the poppy seed-heads to the top edge of the basket. You will need:

Floral foam
1 small, heart-shaped basket
Enough dried poppy seed-heads to go
right around the top edge
Two bunches of dried marjoram flowers

Cut the foam to fit inside the basket and come a little below the level of the basket. Glue each poppy seed-head to the top edge of the basket, working in one direction only. Now take small bunches of the marjoram, and push them into the foam to completely cover the whole basket. Aim to make a really dense mass of flowers, so that no foam shows through. The marjoram should be lower than the poppy seed-heads.

Eucalyptus

LEFT: *The heart-shaped basket really makes this arrangement special – perfect as a centerpiece for a Valentine's Day celebration. Look out for interesting baskets to use.*

Eucalyptus Leaf Garland

*T*o make lengths of leaf garland, all you need to do is:

1 *Pick leaves off branches of fresh eucalyptus.*

2 *Thread them onto flexible wire. Hang them somewhere warm and airy, and they will dry very quickly. Re-thread them onto string or wire again, this time closer together. You can also add other ingredients or different types of leaves between the eucalyptus. Try dried flower heads or green and red apple rings.*

BELOW: *Make alternative garlands to this eucalyptus leaf example by combining herb leaves with other elements, for instance bay leaves and red chilies or dried orange or lemon peel.*

Decorating with Herbs

WREATHS AND GARLANDS
Pages 124-129

DECORATIVE HERB BUNDLES
Pages 130-135

GARDEN POTS AND CONTAINERS
Pages 136-143

INDOOR HERBS
Pages 144-151

WOODEN OUTDOOR CONTAINERS
Pages 152-159

CHRISTMAS HERB DECORATIONS
Pages 160-167

Wreaths and Garlands

Wreaths and garlands of flowers and foliage have become very popular over the last few years. Garlands made from dried material, in particular, make wonderfully decorative additions to the house, where they can be hung formally on a door or wall or hooked more casually across the corner of a bedhead, mirror, or item of furniture. Some kinds are very quick to make and require only small amounts of ingredients, so they are excellent for decorations which are needed in a hurry when something a little more festive and special than an ordinary arrangement is the order of the day.

Herbs, both fresh and dried, make marvellous ingredients for wreaths. Their scent is, of course, an added bonus to the finished item, and many of the flowering herbs are very pretty in their own right as cut flowers. You have a choice of how to construct your wreath. There are many ready-made wreath bases available. These are usually made from grapevine twigs or stems twisted into a ring. They are good-looking enough to use on their own but they can also be used as a base to which other plant material can be attached. This is done by gluing dried stems to the twigs, or wiring in fresh stems, or even by just pushing flowers and foliage among the twigs.

Then there are simple foam rings designed for dried flowers, to be either glued or pushed into place, and plastic-backed foam rings, which can be soaked in water and used for fresh flowers and herbs. These are easy to use and give a very professional effect, though you do need plenty of material to cover the base, as they must be closely packed with flowers, without any foam showing through.

Many different herbs are suitable for using to make wreaths and garlands, including lavender, roses, sage, thyme, rosemary, bay, and many of the shrubbier kinds of herbs with woody stems.

Lavender

RIGHT: Herb-decorated wreaths and garlands make such versatile decorations - as simple and spontaneous as a few bunches of herbs tucked into a twig ring, or as elegant as a wreath of fresh, full-blown roses and summer flowering herbs for a special occasion.

Rose and Golden Marjoram Garland

*T*his is a fresh flower-and-herb garland built up on a moist, floral-foam wreath. Make sure that the foam is thoroughly wetted before inserting the flowers, though it should not be too saturated. Check any instructions that may have come with it for the exact length of soaking time, since these may vary. Work outdoors or on a waterproof surface because as you push the stems into place, the foam usually drips quite a lot. This garland is intended for making when roses are plentiful, in early summer. The varieties used here are 'Charles de Mills' and *Rosa gallica officinalis* or the 'Apothecary's Rose'.

Golden marjoram is a useful, highly decorative, and hardy garden plant. The leaves emerge in spring as a bright lime-green color and if grown in a partly shaded place, this fresh color is maintained all summer, or it may fade slightly to a less bright, but still golden, green.

1 Soak the foam ring ready for use and collect all the plant material. The items used here are golden marjoram, deep pink roses, rosemary, and lavender, with some small-leaved, evergreen leaves, such as wintergreen, juniper, live-oak, or eucalyptus, as a filler.

2 Cut all the plant stems short and start to make the garland by putting marjoram, sprigs of rosemary, and the evergreen leaves all over the foam, working around it systematically until the whole ring is well-covered. Now add the roses and lavender, spacing them evenly throughout the foliage.

ABOVE: *Attach a loop of wire or string if you wish, from which to hang the wreath when it is finished. It will keep fresh for several days, especially if it is sprayed occasionally with water from a plant-mister.*

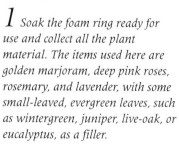

Golden marjoram

Dried Roses on Willow Wreath

Create a small bunch of dried roses and wire them together. Cut the stems very short. Wire them to a wreath made of pale-colored green branches and attach a wide, wire-edged ribbon beside the roses.

RIGHT: *A flamboyant ribbon adds the finishing touch to this pretty wreath. Wire-edged ribbon is wonderful to use in floral decorations, since it can be molded into soft, flowing shapes.*

Lavender Wreath

*T*his pretty and informal wreath makes use of a ready-made vine-twig ring and several different varieties of lavender. As the lavender stems are not kept moist in any way, they will slowly wilt, and then dry out naturally. However, the wreath will look pretty for a special occasion, and could subsequently be air-dried to keep for use as a dried decoration.

If you have a grapevine or other strong vine growing in your garden, it is possible to make your own wreaths. The vine should be harvested as the leaves drop in the fall but while the stems are still pliable. They can then be cut, and long lengths twisted around and around, and the loose ends tucked under each other. You may need to hold the stems together in places with a little thin wire, discreetly placed so as to make it invisible. It is best to make the ring around a cylindrical shape of some kind, so that you get a perfect circle. Leave the vine ring to dry out naturally, and then decorate it how you like, with dried or fresh material.

1 *Collect several different types and colors of fresh lavender, ensuring that the flower heads have stems that are as long as possible.*

2 *Work around the garland in one direction, tucking little bunches of two or three stems of lavender at a time under the vine twigs. Lavender stems are quite bendable and will generally thread fairly easily. If you have problems, then tie them in with small pieces of thin wire.*

3 *Continue around the garland, adding lavender bunches, and varying the colors as you go. Do not aim to cover the twigs completely with flowers. Finish off with a little bow of narrow purple ribbon, and a loop from which to hang the wreath.*

Feverfew

Fresh Herb Bunch on a Twig Ring

*T*his makes the most of the decorative qualities of the ring itself which just has a tiny bunch of fresh herbs added to it. The finished ring could be hung, or would look great as a table decoration for a summer meal outdoors.

You can make a small posy from whatever herbs you have at hand which are pretty and decorative. As previously suggested, the posy could later be hung up in a warm, dry place to air-dry. The herbs could then be used in cooking or potpourris, as appropriate.

Lavender

1 Gather together all the herbs you want to use. Shown here are feverfew, golden marjoram, santolina, and lavender.

2 Tie the stems of the herbs with a small length of raffia or colored twine, and then attach this to the ring at an angle.

Decorative Herb Bundles

*t is a traditional sight in summer wherever scented herbs are grown to see bunches of them, such as lavender, harvested and hung up to dry. They are dried in this way because it is practical and easy, but of course it also happens to be very decorative. Using this functional idea as a starting point, all kinds of pretty and unusual versions of a tied bundle can be made from fresh or dried herbs. You can make bundles which stand upright like small wheat-sheaves, if you make them thick enough at the base to support themselves without any help, or tie bunches of a single type of herb, or pretty mixtures of herbs, to hang singly or in groups.

Bundles made from fresh herbs should be stood in water to make them last more than a few hours, or they can be hung in the fresh air to dry just as they are. Bundles made from dried herbs are generally simple to create, needing only patience to organize the stems and get them to equal lengths, with the flowers or leaves in a neat arrangement above them. Bundles can be further decorated with ribbons, bows, coarse string, or raffia, or whatever takes your fancy. You can add other ingredients such as cinnamon sticks, or little bunches of dried fruits or spices. Whether fresh or dry, the plants you use will need to have straight, stiff stems to stand on their own unless you are going to bind them very tightly with something which will add strength – such as a thick twig or small stick, placed centrally and well-hidden by the stems – in which case you can then use weaker-stemmed materials.

RIGHT: These decorative bunches offer a creative way of displaying all kinds of herbs. Try placing a fragrant bundle in a hallway, where the scent will be able to circulate.

Lavender

Use the finished bundles as decorations anywhere in the house. A pair of dried herb sheaves would look elegant at either end of a mantelpiece or on a shelf, flanking a pretty ornament or picture frame. A single bundle can be tucked among cherished possessions on a display cabinet or low table, and scented versions are delightful on a dressing-table or bedside table. Some bundles are more suitable for hanging in the kitchen, particularly if they are made from the culinary herbs such as bay, rosemary, sage, or thyme.

Dried Lavender Bundle

*D*ried lavender is available in small bunches from dried-flower suppliers, craft stores, and florists. The type sold is usually a dark, purple-flowered type, often from a dwarf variety, and hence the stems are never very long. This doesn't normally matter, but try to get the longest stems possible otherwise you may end up discarding some which are too short. The length of stem is important to the overall proportions of the finished bundle and the bare stems should ideally be about one-and-a-half times to twice the length of the flowered part.

1 You will need several small bunches of lavender to make one bundle. You will also need wire or string for tying and mauve, wire-edged ribbon.

Lavender

2 Unwrap the lavender bunches and discard any stems which are too short or damaged.

3 Begin to re-make a bunch, keeping the flower heads together and at the same level. Don't worry about the stems so much at this stage.

4 When you have made a bunch large enough, tie it tightly halfway between the flowers and stem bases. Now trim the stems so that they are perfectly even, and the bundle will stand on its own. Finish with mauve, wire-edged ribbon.

Cinnamon and Rose Sheaf

*T*his is another dried bundle in a slightly different style. It makes use of deliciously scented cinnamon sticks to make the base, as rose stems are thin and often not very straight. You could add extra scent to the bundle by sprinkling some essential oils onto the flowers and seed-heads. A pair of these sheaves would look lovely in winter as a mantelshelf decoration. The ribbon you choose can change the look of the bundle completely. A red-and-gold one like the one used here looks traditional and even festive, while a plain red or ginger-colored ribbon would look more everyday in style. You will need about:

12 small poppy seed-heads
Thin wire
25 small dried red roses
12 cinnamon sticks, all the same length
Ribbon

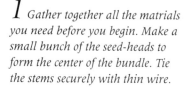

1 Gather together all the matrials you need before you begin. Make a small bunch of the seed-heads to form the center of the bundle. Tie the stems securely with thin wire.

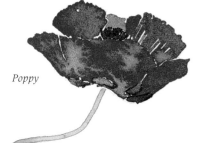

Poppy

ABOVE: A very elegant dried bundle, this cinnamon and rose sheaf would make a memorable gift for a special friend.

Rosemary, Marjoram, and Thyme Bundle

*T*his bundle is made in a slightly different way, as it is designed to be seen from the front, so that the three herbs are layered one above the other. Of course, it is quite difficult to make natural plants perfectly symmetrical but try with this to make it as neat and organized as the herbs will allow. You will need a small bunch of straight-stemmed rosemary, flowering marjoram, and shrubby thyme (not the creeping variety which would be too short). Lay the marjoram on the rosemary, leaving the rosemary projecting about 2 inches above the flowers. Now place the thyme beneath the marjoram. Tie all the stems together, then trim them off to the same length all over, so that they stand on their own. Wrap a narrow leaf, such as an iris or lily leaf, around the wire or string used to tie the stems, to conceal it, or try using grass, green tissue, or natural green raffia for binding.

2 *Add roses around the poppies, framing them neatly, and wire the stems again to hold everything tight. Cut the stems shorter than the cinnamon sticks.*

3 *Put the cinnamon sticks around the stems with the tops quite high up under the flowers. Tie these tightly with wire. Cover the wire with a pretty bow.*

Garden Pots and Containers

Perhaps the best way to grow herbs in a garden is in pots and containers of all kinds. It means that even the smallest city yard or patio can have at least a few leaves of something delicious for the kitchen, or a decorative mixture of herbs to look at. It is possible to appreciate all the wonderful textures and shapes of herb foliage, and the colors and scents of the plants when they are grown in this way. Bringing them up above ground level, too, means that you are tempted to pinch a leaf as you pass, or release the scent as you brush near the leaves.

It is important, when mixing herbs together in one container, that you choose compatible plants, unless you are only aiming for a short-term display. Shrubby herbs, such as thyme, which love good drainage and enjoy the sunlight, will not be too happy combined with a water-loving mint. In the main, though, most herbs are quite easy to cultivate and will survive together because they are basically hardy and good-natured plants. Take care not to plant very large herbs, such as lovage or angelica, in a small container which they might quickly outgrow. On the other hand, a container can be a good way of keeping a rampant herb in check. Mints, for example, are notoriously rapid spreaders, and could take over wherever they are planted, but grown in a container their roots are safe from causing harm to other, smaller plants.

Porous clay and ceramic pots always look good planted with herbs and they are long-lasting and age well, providing that they are frostproof. Plastic never looks so good, but it can mean you spend less time watering plants in the summer, because the soil in them will not dry out as fast as that in porous containers. If you use porous clay pots then it is best to use heavier soil and potting mixtures, rather than soil-free types which can dry out very fast and are difficult to rehydrate.

Sage

RIGHT: A glorious grouping of herb-planted pots and containers offers so many good things – an attractive outdoor display, wonderful scents and a ready source of natural flavorings and garnishes for use in the kitchen.

Various herbs, including rosemary, some lavenders, and lemon verbena, may need to be brought into a frost-free environment if you live in an area with harsh winters, so they can be planted in decorative pots without fear of the containers being damaged by frost.

Containers can be planted with color in mind, or for culinary purposes. They may be a collection of plants which need similar conditions, or just a lovely mixture of scents. Another big advantage to planting herbs in pots is that they can be moved around the garden, or grouped with other containers to make an ever-changing display. The four ideas here are designed first and foremost to look good, concentrating on interesting mixtures of leaf color and shape.

Thyme with Pebbles

*T*hyme loves sunlight and good drainage, and the various varieties are very happy growing between fieldstones. Re-create these conditions in a pot with a covering of fine pebbles over the surface of the soil. This planting uses a shallower pot, as the plants are not very deep-rooting. Use an upright thyme such as this silver, variegated variety, or choose a creeping kind, and then use finer gravel as the soil covering.

1 Put a shallow layer of pebbles or gravel at the base of the pot for drainage. Fill the pot nearly full with a packaged soil mix to which you have added a couple of tablespoons of gravel or perlite.

2 Plant one or two thyme plants, depending upon their size.

Thyme

3 Scatter a layer of tiny pebbles or gravel over the surface, being careful not to damage the plants which will eventually grow and spread out to fill the pot.

RIGHT: *Sage provides a good contrast in leaf size and shape to the small-leaved thyme. Here, variegated varieties of both herbs are combined to great effect.*

Mediterranean Mixture

*T*his is a combination of herbs which is especially good for a sunny site. Combine French lavender with dwarf English lavender and purple-flowered heliotrope (*Heliotropium peruviana*, sometimes called cherry pie because of its scent). Use a well-drained soil or compost and, at the end of the summer, move the pot into a greenhouse or shelter it from frost in some other way. Replace the heliotrope each year, or try using other herbs combined with the lavenders.

LEFT: *Lavender is a herb of Mediterranean origins and the fields of lavender found in the south of France are a breathtaking sight. There are many different varieties of lavender to choose from.*

ABOVE: *Another herb planting featuring the striking French lavender, superbly set off by the blue hue of the container – a demonstration of what a difference your choice of pot can make.*

Bronze and Purple Herb Pot

*U*se a packaged potting mixture containing one-third soil, mixed with a lighter, soil-free potting medium containing peat and perlite. The soil-free mixture alone will be too light and dry out very quickly. For this mixture you will need:

1 violet-colored, glazed ceramic container
Potting mixture
Crushed gravel for drainage
2 bronze fennel plants
2 purple basil plants
1 purple-and-cream variegated sage plant

1 Line the bottom of the container with a layer of gravel or something similar, to provide some drainage for the pot.

2 Add the potting mixture about three-quarters of the way up the pot.

3 Plant the taller bronze fennels at the back, then add the basils, and finally the sage. Basils are annual plants and will need to be replaced each year, while the fennel and sage are perennial. If you live in an area where the winters are long and cold, bring these plants indoors or into a glasshouse when the nights become frosty.

RIGHT: A mixed planting of herbs with colorful foliage makes an effective contrast to combinations of flowering herbs in neighboring pots. Look out for unusual herb varieties at nurseries.

Pineapple mint

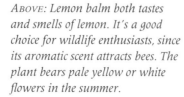

Lemon balm

ABOVE: *Lemon balm both tastes and smells of lemon. It's a good choice for wildlife enthusiasts, since its aromatic scent attracts bees. The plant bears pale yellow or white flowers in the summer.*

RIGHT: *Even if you have a ground-planted herb garden, an attractive pot of herbs can make an impressive focal point within the garden, especially planted with golden-leaved herbs.*

142

Golden-Leaved Herbs in a Container

Lemon balm

This mixture will keep its fresh leaf color through the summer. Stand it out of the sunlight, as this will help to keep the colors fresh. Golden-leaved herbs prefer shade or semi-shade best. For this planting you will need:

1 tall ceramic pot in a greenish-brown glaze
2 golden lemon balm plants
1 lemon-flowered santolina
1 cream variegated sage

1 Put a layer of gravel, pebbles, or pieces of broken terracotta flowerpot in the base of the container for drainage.

2 Fill with a good soil-based potting mixture.

3 Plant the two balms at the back, the santolina to one side, and the sage on the other. Fill with more soil if necessary. Water well.

143

Indoor Herbs

*M*any people have no garden or yard, or have no desire to do any outdoor gardening. Herbs are the perfect plants for growing indoors, because they can be both useful and decorative. Many supermarkets these days sell little growing pots of herbs to snip and use in cooking, and since they are growing, they remain fresh for as long as you need them. However, it is more economical to raise your own plants from seed. Many herbs are easy to cultivate in this way, but for indoor gardening, where conditions are never absolutely perfect, it is probably better to start off with good, well-grown young herb plants, which you can buy from a nursery or garden center. You will also be able to grow more unusual varieties.

Most herbs will require plenty of light and moisture. Do not attempt to grow herbs if you cannot provide natural light for most of the day They can be placed in or near a window as long as they won't get too much direct sunlight at the hottest times of the day during the summer. But even winter sun can occasionally be damaging to tender plants. A very dry atmosphere is not good for many plants, though some, such as scented geraniums, are not bothered by these conditions. The chances are that your indoor herb-garden will end up in the kitchen, and this is probably the most suitable place for it.

Take care and trouble in choosing or decorating special containers or devise ways to display herbs more unconventionally than in a row on the windowsill. Try hanging pots from wires, or planting herbs in hanging baskets, or fixing glass shelves across a window which is not often opened and which doesn't receive much direct sunlight. Keep plants moist but not overwatered, and use clean rainwater rather than water from the faucet, to which plants may react badly if used exclusively.

Parsley

RIGHT: It is easy and rewarding to create a herb display indoors, but like most plants, herbs need a certain amount of attention to keep them in good condition.

144

Feed healthy, growing indoor herbs with liquid fertilizer every week during the summer months. Don't be afraid to trim them often, and pinch out growing tips to encourage them to bush out, since herbs grown indoors can get a little tall and stringy. Certain plants, such as basil and geranium, positively thrive on being trimmed regularly. It is important to keep basil from flowering so that it will continue to produce plenty of new leaves. Once it has been allowed to flower, it will give up, thinking it has done its job.

If you do have a yard or garden, but still like to grow herbs indoors, you can give plants the occasional vacation outside during the summer. This will boost their growth and health. They can then be brought back in again when the weather turns cooler.

Curly-leaved parsley

Hanging Wire Pot-holder

*F*or this idea, you will need some green, plastic-coated wire which is strong, but flexible enough to bend with pliers quite easily. Once you have tried to make one of these, you can experiment with different variations on the same theme.

1 Decide on the pot and plant for which you are going to make the hanger, as it should be made to fit. Have some wire-cutters and pliers ready, and the roll of green wire.

2 Make a circle of wire to fit around the top of the pot, just below the ledge. Make three loops by twisting the wire in three places, equally spaced around the ring.

Join the ends by twisting the wires together. Cut three lengths of wire to make the hangers, and a shorter piece for the top loop.

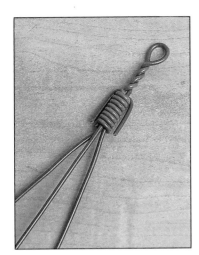

3 Attach the three straight pieces of wire to each loop in the ring, and bring them together at the top.

4 Twist them together and make a loop with the smaller piece of wire, twisting it into a neat spiral. Drop the pot into the ring, and hang it from another piece of wire, threaded through the top loop.

RIGHT: The ever-popular, curly-leaved parsley is treated to a rather more creative method of display than in a pot on a windowsill. The pot-holder is simple to make and natural in its effect.

Basils in a Basket

Basil plants thrive equally well indoors and outdoors, if you live in a warm part of the country. They also respond well to feeding with a liquid fertilizer; use one created especially for houseplants. Plants need plenty of moisture to keep them growing fast and producing lots of lush leaves. Pick out any flower buds, to induce more leaf production.

Purple basil

2 *Cut a piece of black plastic the same shape as the basket base but a little larger all around. Put it into the bottom of the basket.*

1 *You will need a basket which is narrow enough to sit on a windowsill, black plastic to line it, and three or more basil plants. Mix purple with green, for a more interesting effect.*

3 *Now simply stand the basil plants close together inside the basket, and put the basket in a window but away from direct sunlight.*

Basil

149

Pigment-Colored Pots

Plain, new, porous clay pots can be made to look far more interesting by coloring them with powdered paint. There are several ways to do this. Where you wish to use the pots once they are colored will determine the materials you use. You can mix the powdered color with linseed oil and paint this mixture onto the pot. The oil soaks into the porous clay and absorbs some of the color. The rest of the pigment stays on the surface and looks very natural, like the normal matt texture of clay. The pigment will wear away slightly with weathering and handling, leaving a lovely surface finish. On indoor pots, this may be a problem, so it is better for pots being used exclusively indoors to mix the powder pigment with a matt PVA paint medium well thinned with water.

1 Mix red and ocher pigments with a little water and PVA paint medium, to create a warm red shade.

2 Paint it over the outside of the pot with a broad sponge.

3 Leave the pot to dry outdoors before planting it. A scented geranium with deep-red flowers is the perfect choice for the painted pot.

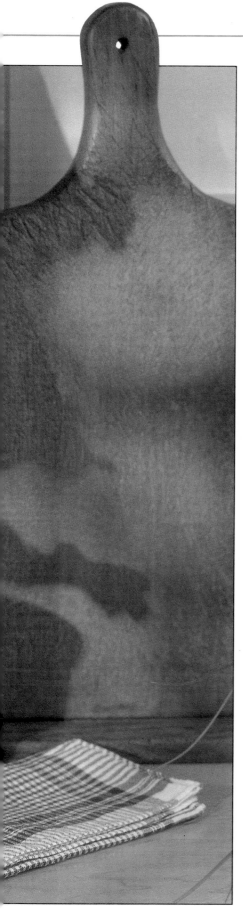

A Painted Trio of Pots

Chives

Painted pots in blue, yellow, and green are used here to contain chives, baby's tears (*Soleirolia soleirolii*) and curly-leaved parsley.

LEFT: *The red of this simply painted, porous clay pot echoes the color of the geranium's flowers, while providing a dramatic contrast to the blue tablecloth.*

ABOVE: *A simple grouping of these brightly colored, pigment-painted pots makes an eye-catching display. Snip off the chive flowers to retain the herb's flavor.*

Wooden Outdoor Containers

Containers for outdoor plantings have been made from wood for as long as people have been gardening. Alongside stone and clay, wood has always been a very important material in garden construction and decoration. Where once woods such as oak and elm would have been used, nowadays softwoods have generally taken their place, especially as people have moved away from the ecologically unsound imported tropical woods, such as teak. Softwoods will never last as long as hardwoods, but they can do a reasonable job outdoors.

If you are planting herbs intended for eating, do not plant them in a wooden container that has been treated with preservatives. It's easy to liven up a plain pine planter with non-toxic paint or stain, if you wish. On the other hand, some handsome woods, such as oak, age and weather to a lovely silver-gray, which may be almost a sacrilege to cover.

There are many special paints designed for outdoor use and specifically for wood, so look out for them. It is fun to match the color of the container with the plants inside, or to choose contrasting or even clashing colors, depending upon how bold you feel and the effect you are after. There is nothing to stop you changing the color of your wooden window boxes every year if you want to. Many paints can be used straight over new or old wood without preparation, primers, or undercoats, and are meant to be micro-porous to let the wood "breathe."

LEFT: Weathered wooden tubs, such as this example, have a charm all of their own and really don't need any dressing up.

RIGHT: Look out for any discarded wooden crates or boxes that would make interesting containers for your herbs, especially when enhanced with colorful paints.

Marjoram

Search out wooden containers which can be recycled from their former use to make attractive planters for herbs. Even if they are short-term, lasting perhaps only for one season, something like a cheap, light wooden crate will still look good with plants growing in it, so don't throw it away. Fruit and vegetables are still packed in wooden trays, which can be painted and used as plant containers for small and shallow-rooted herbs, such as varieties of thyme. Use your initiative, and try anything which could conceivably be adapted easily to hold plants. An empty wooden wine, or whiskey barrel, cut in half, is still one of the best of all containers for displaying plants, and is large enough to have quite a good-sized and well-established herb garden growing in it for many years. In this case, it is definitely more handsome if it is left in its natural wood color.

A Collection of Thymes in a Fruit Box

ABOVE: Common thyme is the culinary variety and a cultivated form of the wild thyme which grows in the mountainous regions of Mediterranean countries.

RIGHT: Different varieties of thyme have varying colors of flowers, from white to crimson, as well as foliage of different hues, including bright green and blue-gray.

*T*his planting uses an ordinary thin wooden fruit box, painted a pretty, soft green to complement the thyme plants inside. When it is planted and the herbs are growing, it would look prettiest put somewhere above the ground, on a table or pedestal of some kind. Thymes like sunlight and good drainage. You will need a wooden fruit box, plastic to line it, suitable matt paint, soil, and thyme plants.

Thyme

1 Use a special exterior paint or wood paint in a matt finish, in a shade of green, to paint the outside of the box and a little way down the inside edges. Leave to dry.

2 Line the base and slightly up the inside edges with a rectangle of black plastic. Puncture tiny holes all over the plastic to allow for drainage.

3 Fill the box with soil that has had some gravel added to it, then plant it with as many small thyme plants as will fit inside. Put the taller ones at the back, and the lower-growing ones at the front.

Fruit Box planted with Scented Geraniums

Pelargonium is the botanic name for the plants we more commonly call geraniums. Scented pelargoniums are lovely plants to grow in a greenhouse, yard, patio, or garden. Each variety has a different scent in its foliage. Many of them have quite insignificant flowers, and are mainly grown for their foliage. For a collection like this one it is good to add a few more showy types of pelargoniums, such as the Uniques or Regals, to provide colorful flowers. Line the fruit box with plastic and fill with good, gravelly soil or packaged potting mixture. Plant a mixture of pelargoniums, and perhaps a lavender or rosemary plant for foliage contrast. Keep this box in a sunny position, and water sparingly but regularly.

LEFT: *Different varieties of scented pelargoniums offer a range of wonderful scents, from the fruity fragrances of apple and orange, to rose-lemon or peppermint.*

ABOVE: *This wooden barrel makes an attractive container for herbs and hostas. Line with plastic that has been pierced to create holes for drainage.*

Viola Basket

A pretty display for spring and early summer made using purple violas is shown here planted in a traditional English wooden, flat-bottomed basket, of the kind known as a trug. A good handmade trug is very expensive and any decorative shallow, woven basket will do. You could even make your own! Once the violas have finished flowering in late summer, re-plant them into a border, to flower the following year. While the plants are in flower, the basket would look very pretty as a focal point on a garden or patio table.

1 Drill small holes in the basket for drainage and treat it with a preservative to prevent it from rotting.

2 Then simply line it with a layer of drainage material and fill it with soil.

3 Plant it with several small viola plants, as if it were a conventional container. Water them well, and top up with more earth if necessary.

Viola

157

Chives

BELOW: *A plain window box sets off a lush mixture of herbs, including thyme, parsley, chives, violas, and nasturtiums.*

Mixed Herbs in a Window-Box

A window box planted with herbs makes a very successful display, as it is possible to use plants that look good all year around. With a basis of perennial herbs permanently planted, you could then add other annual varieties or flowers to bring color. For spring color, you could plant small bulbs with the herbs, to come up and flower through and between the herb plants. A soft blue paint color is a very sympathetic choice to complement the herbs inside. Use a matt paint for the most subtle finish. The window box below contains a variety of herbs, including French sorrel (*Rumex scutatus*), golden thymes, variegated sage, and marjoram.

French sorrel

RIGHT: *Here, sage, lavender, and scented geraniums are cleverly combined with strawberry plants for a really luscious display.*

BELOW: *Ideally, French sorrel should be grown in full sun, in a rich, well-drained soil.*

Christmas Herb Decorations

Christmas is a wonderful time to display your creativity with herbs, incorporating them into homemade decorations. Quite a few herbs are still green and fragrant through the winter, especially if you live in the South or the Southwest. The glossy leaves of boxwood and bay are in fine condition to make into decorations, and rosemary is often in flower through milder spells of winter weather in warmer parts of the country. Thymes are evergreen, too, though they may not be as pungent in scent during the winter as they are in the summer. In colder regions you can use dried herbs, many of which are quite decorative.

Natural decorations at Christmas are always prettier than artificial ones, and if you are well-prepared you can have all kinds of lovely ingredients to use. Collect leaves in the fall and press them flat and dry, and pick berries on the stem and allow them to dry naturally. Dried roses and other summer flowers can add any color you may need and silver-and-white dried flowers and foliage bring a touch of glitter and frost. Combine these with spices and other scented items, such as dried and fresh citrus peels, eucalyptus leaves, nuts in their shells, popcorn, seed-heads, and fruits. If you want to make everything look a little more glamorous, then you can add touches of silver and gold with paint, spray, or gold- and silver-leaf. Keep this to a minimum, or it will overpower the subtle prettiness of the natural items.

The most effective kinds of decorations are often the simplest in concept, so don't try to make anything which is too complicated or contrived. Tiny bunches of dried flowers and herbs make charming Christmas tree decorations, either wired into place, or tied with thin gold cord or ribbon to the branches. A tree completely covered in these little posies would look quite spectacular, or they could be used among other, more conventional, decorations.

RIGHT: Bring the magic of herbs to your festive decorations this year. Rosemary (the symbol of friendship), with its pungent, piney smell, makes a delightful substitute for the more predictable Christmas greenery.

Thyme

Table settings for the Christmas festivities can benefit from the herb treatment too. A simple pyramid of fresh fruits, shiny red apples, lemons, or oranges, looks magnificent when spiked with sprays of glossy bay leaves. Or tiny bunches of fresh herbs can be tied onto a napkin for each guest. Dried red roses and fresh rosemary would make beautiful posies to decorate each place-setting, especially if they were standing in small red glasses. The possibilities are endless once the imagination gets going, so consider using herbs, both fresh and dried, for the next festive season.

Pomegranate Pyramid

*P*omegranates are wonderfully festive, with their spectacular rich-red-and-coral coloring, and pretty shapes. Nothing could be simpler than making a pile of these fruits, and contrasting them with a few pieces of evergreen herb, such as wintergreen or juniper, or citrus leaves, from Florida or California, which are at their best in the winter. After you have finished the decoration, leave the pomegranates in a warm, airy place to dry naturally. They can then be used for other decorations later. You will need:

8 pomegranates
Glass-stemmed dish
Small red apples and/or berries
Bunch of fresh evergreens
Bunch of fresh rosemary

2 First pile the pomegranates onto the dish. Arrange the apples and berries in between.

Rosemary

1 Gather your ingredients together. Polish the fruits with a soft cloth.

3 Cut leaves of evergreen and push between the fruits. Do the same with small sprigs of rosemary.

Tree Decorations

Small bunches to tie to the tree are quick and easy to make and, if stored carefully, can be used year after year. If the rosemary is fresh, it will dry naturally while it is on the tree. Add a few drops of essential oil to the decorations if you wish. You will need:

Fresh or dried rosemary
Dried gypsophila (baby's-breath)
Small red dried roses
Dried cornflowers or other blue flowers
Thin wire

2 Lay two or three sprigs of rosemary on the working surface. Add a sprig of gypsophila (baby's-breath).

3 Add a few roses and blue flowers to make an elegant spray.

1 Gather all the ingredients together. Cut the lavender and gypsophila (baby's-breath) into small sprigs, and place in separate piles for easy access. Trim the rose stems.

4 Tie the stems together with wire, to make a little fan-shaped spray of flowers. Leave a length of wire long enough to attach the spray to the Christmas tree.

Herb-Decorated Candles

*I*t is lovely to light the house with plenty of candlelight at Christmastime. Use large, slow-burning candles and attach small bunches or sprigs of herbs to each. Tie with a richly colored festive ribbon. Never leave a lighted candle unattended in case it burns down too quickly.

ABOVE: These pretty little sprays of flowers and herbs could also be used to decorate mirrors or picture frames, or napkins for a festive table setting.

RIGHT: A collection of candles of varying sizes, similarly adorned with bunches of herbs, would make an atmospheric and aromatic table centerpiece for a festive feast.

165

Conical Boxtree

This little tree can be made any size you like. If it is hard to find boxwood, use any other fresh or dried small-leaved evergreens, such as juniper or wintergreen. If you prefer, the tree foliage can simply stand straight on a surface, without a stem, in a pot. You will need:

Boxwood branches
Glue-gun
Cone-shaped floral foam
Short length of branch for tree trunk
Porous clay pot
Floral foam to fill the pot
Reindeer moss

1 Cut the boxwood branches into small, manageable sprigs. Heat up the glue-gun.

Box

2 Working from the base of the cone, glue the sprigs of boxwood to the foam, working around systematically, and aiming to completely cover the foam.

3 When the cone is covered with leaves, cut a small hole from the base to fit the trunk. Glue the trunk to the base. Fill the pot with foam and push the trunk into place. Decorate with real or artificial fruit and perhaps place a bauble on the top of the tree. Cover the foam in the pot with small pieces of reindeer moss.

167

Herbs for Health and Beauty

BATH OILS, SCRUBS, AND GELS
Pages 170-175

COLOGNES AND FRAGRANCES
Pages 176-183

HANDS AND FEET
Pages 184-189

FACE AND SKIN
Pages 190-195

HERBS FOR THE HAIR
Pages 196-201

Bath Oils, Scrubs, and Gels

While bathing has always been a functional routine with its primary purpose to cleanse the body, it nevertheless has connotations of pleasure and relaxation. Once we discovered that bathing could be a pleasurable experience, coinciding, no doubt, with the means of getting large enough quantities of hot water easily, we found ways of making it even more enjoyable and beneficial to the body and mind. Scent, in particular, has the ability to soothe and relax us. From earliest times all kinds of ingredients have been added to bathwater in order to smooth and cleanse the skin, replenish lost moisture, or simply to soften and perfume the water. Herbs and flowers have traditionally played a central role in this ritual, from the days of the rose-scented baths enjoyed by the Romans to today's invigorating scrubs and gels.

Making your own ingredients for pleasing bathtimes is not difficult. It can be as simple as diluting some deliciously scented essential oils into a hot bath to making special scrubs or little sachets to run under the faucet. Many commercial bath additives are very harsh, as they are based on detergents which strip the skin of oils, while providing the foam that people seem to like. Few of them actually moisturize. Raw oatmeal is useful for softening and gently cleansing the skin. A small cheesecloth bag of raw oatmeal agitated through the warm bathwater makes a lovely silky bath to soak in. Add herbs, rose petals, and scents of other kinds, and you have a truly delicious mixture.

RIGHT: Making your own bath additives is as simple as it is pleasurable. What's more, these natural preparations will help to soothe your skin, relax frayed nerves, and invigorate your body.

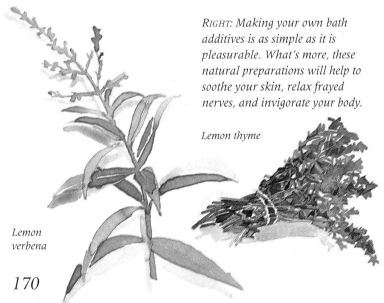

Lemon thyme

Lemon verbena

The traditional bathtime herbs have been rosemary, lavender, and rose. You can experiment with different ingredients to achieve the scents and skin-treating properties you are aiming for. In many recipes, you can use dried herbs very successfully and in smaller quantities than you would need for fresh herbs, but if you have access to fresh herbs then make good use of them, remembering to boost the quantities by at least twice as much. Most of the ingredients for these recipes are available from pharmacies if you ask for them, but you can also find them in specialty stores, such as herbalists, and some health food stores. Many of them are surprisingly inexpensive, compared with commercially made bath additives.

Herb Bubble Bath Gel

Pure or castile soap for making this gel can be bought from good pharmacies. It contains no scent or other additives.

1 cup water
1 tbsp sweet woodruff
1 tbsp mint
1 tbsp comfrey
1 tbsp angelica
5 tbsps pure soap
2 tbsps glycerine
2 tsps witch hazel
5 drops oil of lemon verbena
1 tbsp unflavored gelatin

Makes about ¾ pint gel

Woodruff

Angelica

LEFT: *This recipe makes a lovely, softening mixture which produces a nice foam if you pour it into the bath before running the water.*

1 *Measure out the ingredients and boil the water.*

2 *Make an infusion of the herbs and the boiling water. Grate the soap.*

Aromatic Bath Oil

*B*ath oils work by settling a film of oil over the surface of the bath. They do not disperse in the water unless they are in an emulsion. They leave the skin feeling very soft and can be perfumed with essential oils. Pat your skin dry after the bath, don't rub it. This mixture can be adapted, of course, by using different essential oils.

½ cup tincture of benzoin
¼ cup avocado oil
10 drops oil of sandalwood
10 drops oil of cinnamon
10 drops oil of orange
10 drops oil of basil
10 drops oil of rosemary

Combine all the ingredients, and shake thoroughly to mix them. Use 1 tablespoon per bath. You can use almond or apricot oil in place of avocado.

3 *Strain the infusion and discard the herbs. Add the soap, stirring well. Combine the glycerine and witch hazel, and add the oil. Add this to the herb mixture.*

4 *When it is all thoroughly mixed, add the gelatin, and stir until it is perfectly dissolved. When cool, transfer the mixture to small jars.*

Herbal Bath Sachets

*T*hese little sachets can be made in quantity, and used one to a bath. Here they are made in a pretty fabric, but for everyday, the herb mixture can simply be spooned into a square of ordinary cheesecloth and tied with string. The cheesecloth can even be re-used once the herbs have lost their properties. To use the sachets, either throw one into the tub and leave it, or hold it under the faucet as the bathwater is run. You may find that it can be used for a second bath. This mixture is wonderfully refreshing and invigorating; change the varieties of herbs in the mixture if you want a different effect. Cup measures are again used here, to ensure the correct proportions.

4 cups dried lemon verbena
2 cups dried thyme
1 cup dried peppermint
Fabric such as organdy or cheesecloth, which
allows the water to penetrate easily

1 Mix the herbs together thoroughly in a bowl. Cut out pieces of fabric to make the sachets. In this case, cut a rectangle which will fold into a square, leaving a little extra to make a turning at the top.

2 With the right sides of the fabric together, sew along the sides. Turn the right way out, and turn down the top edge to neaten. Sew this in place. Fill with the herb mixture, and tie the bag together with ribbon or cord.

Bath Scrub

This mixture is designed to be rubbed briskly onto damp skin before bathing, then rinsed off. The oatmeal smoothes and softens the skin beautifully, and the thyme is marvellously refreshing and astringent. The orange and rose provide the delicious scent. To make this, you need a small coffee-grinder or spice-grinder, so that you can obtain a fine powder from the various ingredients.

3 cups coarse oatmeal
1 cup dried, scented, red rose petals
1 cup dried thyme
Dried orange peel from 2 oranges

1 Measure out and prepare the ingredients. Choose a suitable, airtight container for the scrub.

2 Work with small batches, grinding a mixture of the different ingredients each time.

3 Finally, mix all the batches you have ground really well together before putting them into an airtight container to store. Store in a cool, dark place.

Thyme

Colognes and Fragrances

$\mathcal{U}$ntil quite recently, no one had thought much about the possibilities of making and creating perfumes and fragrances at home. Now that it is so much easier to buy natural essential oils, there is really no difficulty in making your own fragrances. They may not have the subtlety of some of the famous name-brands from Parisian perfumeries which have access to fabulous ingredients from around the world, but they can be fresh and delightful, and will cost a fraction of the price of commercial perfumes.

While perfumes might not have been homemade, refreshing colognes and scented waters have a long history, from the simple rosewater splashed over a weary visitor upon arrival at a house in Medieval times, to the delicate lavender-scented toilet waters and colognes of the last century. Perfumes were often considered too sophisticated – even wicked! – to many people with strict religious codes, but colognes were simple and wholesome, and were therefore permitted for refreshing hot brows, dabbing inside wrists, and sprinkling on handkerchiefs on summer days.

Always use totally pure essential oils, and be sure that they have not been diluted or tampered with in any way. Buy from a reputable herbalist who guarantees the authenticity of the product. A good way of checking is to see whether the oils vary in price. Some fragrances are more costly than others to collect and produce. If they are all being sold at the same price, the expensive oils are unlikely to be pure.

Rosemary

RIGHT: Fragrances and perfumes are easy and inexpensive to create at home. They make excellent gifts for friends and family, presented in attractive bottles, trimmed with ribbon or small sprays of mixed dried herbs.

A few people have an allergic or negative reaction to certain oils applied directly to the skin. In most fragrances and colognes, the oils are very diluted, but always be careful when using a mixture for the first time. Some substances, such as bergamot (oswego or bee-balm), can provoke an allergenic reaction on the skin, even when diluted. Test it out on yourself first, and do not give it to anyone unless you are sure they will not be harmed by it. Oil of bergamot (oswego or bee-balm) is not to be confused with oil of the bergamot orange, which is used extensively in perfumery. The scents are very similar, hence the name, but oil from the orange is not allergenic.

Once you have tried mixing and making your own fragrances, you may find that you wish to experiment further, creating your own personal perfumes. This can be a fascinating subject, and also a perfect means of making very special gifts for friends and relations. Look out for second-hand bottles in which to store your creations, or save your old bottles that once contained perfumes. It is possible to buy some beautiful new bottles and containers for storing fragrances, but remember that they must have a completely airtight stopper if the contents are not to evaporate. Keep the fragrances in a cool and preferably a dark place, if you wish to store them for any length of time. It is not possible to buy pure alcohol these days to use as a base for perfumes and colognes, although you may find it in good pharmacies in Mexico and Europe. Make sure you are allowed to bring it into the country! The nearest substitute is vodka, which has no smell of its own. Most recipes are easy to make, but time is needed for the ingredients to blend and mature. Check the time required before making a recipe.

Bergamot

RIGHT: *You can be quite generous in applying this citrusy splash – it is lovely as an astringent on a hot summer's day. Ideally, you would need to make this fragrance a few months in advance if you plan to make a gift of it, to allow the scent to mature fully.*

Orange and Lemon Verbena Splash

*T*his is a fresh and zesty splash-on fragrance for use after a bath or shower. Orangeflower water is available at specialty food stores and good pharmacies.

1 unwaxed or organic orange
1 unwaxed or organic lemon
1 cup dried lemon verbena
2¼ cups vodka
⅔ cup orangeflower water
10 drops oil of orange
10 drops oil of lemon verbena
5 drops oil of bergamot
5 drops oil of rose geranium

Makes about ¾ pint

1 Gather together and measure out the ingredients you need, and select a suitable, airtight bottle for storing the fragrance. Rinse and dry the fruits.

Lemon verbena

2 Peel the orange and lemon, and put the peel with the lemon verbena into the alcohol. Stir well, cover with plastic wrap, or pour into a screw-top jar, and leave for about a week, shaking occasionally.

3 Strain the mixture and discard the herbs and peels.

4 Add the orangeflower water and the essential oils. Stir very thoroughly. Bottle and store for as long as possible, but do not use for at least 2 months.

Rose and Vanilla Perfume

This is a rich, sweet perfume, very feminine and delicious. Oil of roses is an expensive essential oil, so you can substitute rose geranium oil if you prefer. Petitgrain oil is used in perfumery and is available from good drugstores and companies that sell essential oils. When using vanilla for cosmetics, always use the pure oil or extract, never the alcohol-based extract used in cooking.

⅓ cup vodka
1 tbsp rosewater
1 cup scented dried rose petals
2 vanilla beans
10 drops oil of roses
10 drops oil of vanilla
10 drops petitgrain oil
5 drops oil of ylang-ylang

Rose

1 Measure out the vodka and the rose petals, or pull the petals off the roses if they are whole. Place the vodka and petals in a glass container.

2 Slightly crush the vanilla pods and steep with the rose petals in the vodka. Cover, and leave for a week.

3 Strain the vodka, and add the rosewater. Stir very well.

4 Add the drops of essential oils, stirring constantly. Bottle and leave to mature about four weeks. Strain again through a filter paper and bottle before using.

Lime Skin Freshener for Men

*T*his is a citrus-based, scented, splash-on cologne to be used on the face or body. The limes must be as fresh as possible, or the oils in the skins will have evaporated. You will need:

2 fresh limes
1 cup vodka
15 drops oil of lime
10 drops petitgrain oil
5 drops oil of lavender
5 drops oil of bergamot
5 drops oil of bayleaf
1 tsp tincture of benzoin
1 cup rosewater

RIGHT: Tincture of benzoin is added to this cologne to act as both a preservative and an astringent. It is also a mild antiseptic.

Bay

1 Gather together all the ingredients and put to one side, except for the vodka and the limes. Measure out the vodka.

2 Peel the limes and put the peel into the vodka. Cover and leave to steep for a week.

Lavender

3 Put the drops of essential oil and the benzoin into the rosewater, and stir very well. Strain the vodka and discard the lime peel. Mix the rosewater with the vodka. Stir very well and bottle. Leave for four weeks. Strain again through a paper filter, then bottle finally before use.

Rosemary

Eau de Cologne

Splash on this cologne generously whenever you need to freshen up. There are several versions of the traditional recipe. Most recipes call for neroli oil which is expensive, but you don't need very much of it.

12 drops oil of bergamot
12 drops oil of lemon
20 drops oil of orange
3 drops neroli oil
3 drops oil of rosemary
2 drops oil of basil
½ cup vodka
2 tbsps spring water

Add the oils to the vodka and stir well. Cover and leave to stand for 48 hours. Add the spring water and stir again. Leave another 48 hours, or up to four weeks if you can wait. Stir and strain through filter paper. Dilute with more water if it seems too strong. Bottle and use.

Hands and Feet

*H*ands and feet are the hard-working parts of our bodies which seem to be the most neglected. While we lavish care and attention on our faces and bodies, our feet, in particular, are often more-or-less ignored. Hands suffer doubly from the normal everyday exposure to the cold and the sun's harmful rays, and alongside this, all the harsh substances, such as detergents, which we use almost without stopping to think of the damage they do. Herbs are extremely helpful in alleviating this damage and in providing some of the luxurious cosmetics that improve the condition of hard-working hands and feet.

For centuries, people have soothed tired and aching feet in a hot footbath scented with herbs and spiced with other ingredients. Peppermint and eucalyptus both have a marvellously invigorating effect on the feet, pepping up the circulation and leaving a warm tingling glow. It is very easy to make a quick footbath at the end of a long day by adding a few drops of essential oil to warm water. Some herbs that are beneficial to the feet are marigold, to help soften hard or calloused skin, and fennel, lavender, and chamomile, to help reduce the swelling in swollen feet. Geranium oil is great for improving the elasticity of skin on the feet, and it boosts the circulation which is important to keep chapped hands at bay during the winter months.

Hands are more likely to need serious nourishment, rather than an invigorating treatment. Nails and cuticles are particular problem areas. Many old-fashioned handcreams were designed to bleach and keep the hands soft and white.

RIGHT: *Herbs have much to offer in being able to nourish hard-working hands and feet, and to heal and protect them, when applied in homemade creams, gels, and baths.*

Rose

184

We are unlikely to worry about freckles much nowadays, but it is sensible to screen the skin on hands from too much sun, as they show signs of aging earlier than any other part of the body. Elderflower and chamomile are traditional herbs for the hands and so are rose, lavender, marigold, and geranium. Combined with rich oils and creams, these can do much to improve the texture of the skin on the hands. If you spend a lot of time doing heavy, messy work, such as gardening, then you will need all the help you can get. Try to remember to wear a barrier cream or salve on the hands before starting work, and use gloves whenever possible. At the end of the day, treat hands to a rich cream, and go to bed wearing cotton gloves.

Almond and Rose Hand Cream

This is quite a thick cream, designed to be slowly massaged into the hands at the end of a hard day. For other times, use a much smaller quantity and rub it in really well until it has been absorbed. Beeswax granules are available from craft stores that specialize in candlemaking, and from beekeepers.

3 tbsps almond oil
3 tbsps coconut oil
2 tbsps white beeswax granules
4 tbsps glycerin
5 drops oil of roses or rose geranium
10 drops evening primrose oil

1 Measure out the ingredients, and fill the lower part of a double-boiler or a saucepan with water. Place over low heat.

2 Melt the almond oil, coconut oil, and beeswax in a bowl over the saucepan of simmering water.

3 Add the glycerin, drop by drop, stirring, until you have a creamy mass.

Rosemary

4 Add the essential oils, beat well, and pour into clean jars.

Sage

LEFT: If you are hard on your hands, it is worth making up several jars of this rich hand cream, so that you can keep a ready supply wherever you wash your hands.

Rosemary, Lavender, and Sage Foot Cream

*T*his is perfect for rough, dry skin on feet. Rub it in well after a softening foot bath. Use beeswax granules if you can find them, as they dissolve much faster than large solid blocks of beeswax, which have to be grated to melt quickly.

2 tbsps white beeswax granules
2 tbsps cocoa butter
6 tbsps apricot kernel oil
10 drops oil of rosemary
10 drops oil of lavender
10 drops oil of sage
15 drops evening primrose oil

Melt the beeswax and cocoa butter in the top half of a double-boiler over boiling water, stirring gently until the wax has dissolved completely. Warm the apricot oil in another small pan and add it slowly to the first mixture, beating constantly. Remove from the heat, and add the essential oils and evening primrose oil. Pour into small jars or tins, and store in a cool, dark place to keep it fresh.

Elderflower and Chamomile Hand Gel

*T*his gentle, soothing yellow gel is excellent for softening hands without making them feel greasy.

½ cup water
2 tbsps dried chamomile
2 tbsps dried elderflowers
3 tbsps glycerin
3 tbsps arrowroot

Chamomile

1 Gather together and measure out the ingredients. Assemble some small screw-top jars for storage.

3 Warm the glycerin in a double-boiler, and add the arrowroot. Stir very well.

LEFT: *Chamomile has many healing and cosmetic uses. This hand gel exploits the herb's ability to soften the skin. Elderflower is effective as a tonic for all skins.*

Walnut, Bay, and Balm Footbath

*M*ake a strong infusion of fresh herbs by steeping about 9 cups of herbs in 1 quart of boiling water. Include the following: English walnut leaves, bay, rosemary, lavender, sage, and lemon balm. If English walnut trees do not grow in your area, use the leaves of butternut, black walnut, or pecan, or you can even substitute wintergreen (checkerberry). Strain the liquid and whisk in a tablespoon of grated castile soap to 1 quart of infusion. Add a few drops of rosemary and bay essential oils, and soak the feet at least 10 minutes. Pat them dry, and rub in some nourishing foot cream or plain almond oil, while the feet are still warm. Put on a pair of clean cotton socks, and sit with your feet up for a while, or go to bed, lying with your feet slightly raised on a pillow.

2 *Heat the water and add the herbs. Leave to steep until thoroughly cooled.*

4 *Strain the infusion. Gradually add to the glycerin and arrowroot mixture, and stir until it is clear and starting to gel. Put into the jars.*

Walnut

Face and Skin

*H*erbs can do wonders for the skin of the face or body. Our skin needs every bit of help it can get, because though many of us eat better food than previous generations our skin is subjected to dangerous sunlight and air pollution from all around us, as well as affected by the strains of a stressful lifestyle. Skin and hair are the first indicators of being out of condition and though we all know we should exercise more, eat healthier foods, drink less alcohol, and get more fresh air, few of us do anything about it!

Herbs play a part in directly healing damaged skin, and a second more subtle role in lifting the spirits and soothing the mind, which greatly affects the way we ultimately look. Many people would rather use products made from plain, wholesome ingredients, and many of the cosmetic and beauty houses are trying to provide these, even in their most high-tech ranges of products.

Many of the simplest and most old-fashioned remedies are the best, for example, rosewater and witch hazel has been used for decades as a mild toner and skin freshener. It could not be easier to make, and is so much less expensive than a commercial alternative. Ingredients for all these recipes are generally available from good pharmacies and drugstores. Very often, they can be ordered for you so you can get ingredients which are not on the shelves. Otherwise, find a herbalist or company which will send ingredients by mail-order. As there is a renewed interest in making cosmetics at home, many ingredients are easier to find than they once were.

RIGHT: Herbs can be used effectively in a whole range of skin preparations, including lotions and creams, astringents and masks, scrubs, cleansers, night and day creams, steam treatments, and compresses.

Making creams and lotions is fun and generally quite easy, though you will improve with practice. Understanding the process of obtaining an emulsion is important. A lotion or cream is an emulsion of various oils in a non-oily base. Often a liquid such as rosewater is added to the melted oils, drop by drop, rather like making mayonnaise. As the water-based liquid meets and mixes with the warm oils, they emulsify and turn opaque and creamy. This is the process which is used for many recipes. It is really fascinating to see it happening the first time. Occasionally things go wrong, usually because temperatures or proportions are not right, but this is quite rare.

Rose and lavender are two herbs that are frequently used for skin preparations, as are marigold, elderflower, and chamomile. Others, from a very long list, include fennel, carrot, and geranium.

Rosewater and Witch Hazel Toner

*H*arsh astringents and toners can do more harm than good, but if you use a cream cleanser, the skin cries out for a cooling tonic to finish. This one is exactly right. It has been used for centuries, and one can see why. Find a source of good-quality rosewater. Often it is sold quite inexpensively at pharmacies and drugstores.

1 tbsp vodka
2 tbsps glycerin
1 cup rosewater
½ cup witch hazel

Mix the vodka with the glycerin and stir very well. Pour into the rosewater and add the witch hazel. Bottle and shake until well blended. Shake the bottle each time before using. Sprinkle on cotton balls and dab gently onto the face.

Simple Mint Cleanser

Eau de cologne mint

This is cooling, soothing and deliciously scented. You can make it in a blender if you prefer. Made this way, even after straining, some tiny shreds of mint may remain in the mixture, so rinse the face well after use. Sprinkle it on a cotton ball and rub it over your skin instead of soap. It is particularly good to use if you have a delicate skin.

2¼ cups fresh milk
4 tbsps fresh mint (apple, eau-de-cologne, or peppermint)

1 Measure out the milk and pour into a clean bowl. Wash the mint and dry.

2 Chop the mint finely, and add it to the milk. Leave to infuse in the refrigerator for about 12 hours.

3 Strain the liquid and bottle it. Store it in the refrigerator.

Applemint

Apricot and Orange Moisturizer

*T*his is a fairly rich cream for the skin of the face or body. If you want to tint it, use a tiny amount of a natural food coloring to make it a pale apricot color. You will need:

2 tsps white beeswax granules
4 tbsps apricot kernel oil
2 tbsps coconut oil
2 tbsps glycerin
2 tbsps orangeflower water
3 drops oil of orange

1 Gather all the ingredients together and measure out the beeswax granules.

2 Melt the beeswax and apricot kernel and coconut oils in the top half of a double-boiler, over hot water, stirring until they are completely dissolved.

LEFT: *Orangeflower water is good for dry skin and stimulates cell replacement.*

3 Add the glycerin to the beeswax and oils, and stir thoroughly. Warm the orangeflower water separately.

4 Remove the double-boiler from the heat and add the orangeflower water, drop by drop, beating all the time, until it is a smooth cream. Add the oil of orange and stir well. Add coloring if you wish. Put into small jars.

ABOVE: *Steam your face for about 10 mintues over the rose or herb infusion of your choice. Then refresh the skin with a clean, damp facecloth. Your skin will feel cleansed and revitalized.*

Fennel

Rose Steam Treatment

One of the simplest of all beauty treatments is a herbal steam bath, to open the pores and deep-cleanse the skin. It is like a sauna for the face, with the added bonus of scented beneficial herbs to do the soothing and healing. If your skin is very blemished or delicate, do not attempt a steam treatment. Normal and oily skins will benefit from regular steam-baths. Simply mix a handful or two of fresh or dried herbs of your choice in a bowl of very hot water. Let them infuse a few seconds, then put your face over them, and cover your head with a towel to keep the heat in. Roses make the most delicious treatment, especially if you can use fresh, highly scented roses from the garden in summer. Alternatively, try basil, chamomile, or marigold, or create a mixture, such as a combination of fennel and lavender.

Herbs for the Hair

While nothing does as much as a good cut for a beautiful head of hair, how you wash it and the products you put on it have a very important effect too. In the days before mass-produced shampoos and conditioners, people had to concoct these things from ingredients found easily in the home and, as in other branches of housekeeping, sensible women turned to herbs. From leaves, stems, and flowers, found wild or cultivated, they made lotions and washes which were functional but which added extra gloss or natural-looking color to the hair. Certain herbs, such as willow, horsetail, rosemary, yarrow, nettle, and chamomile, have always been connected with healthy hair and scalp.

These days, we wash our hair more frequently than our ancestors did, and need to take special care of its condition. To ensure you have the glossiest hair, wash it in a gentle shampoo, and rinse and rinse until no trace is left. Restoring a slightly acidic balance to the hair after using alkaline products is another key factor in improving its look. Of course, it goes without saying that a healthy lifestyle and good diet will do more for the hair from the inside than anything applied from the outside.

At one time, it was thought that certain herbs could cure baldness and increase the growth of hair. It is highly unlikely that anything was really able to do this, but certain herbs definitely stimulate the blood circulation to the skin of the scalp and perhaps have led to the belief that the hair was growing more luxuriantly. Most men these days use the same kinds of hair products as women do, but a century or two ago there were all manner of special brilliantines, pomades, tonics, and rubs for the man who cared about his appearance.

Soapwort

RIGHT: Treat your hair and scalp to the attention they deserve by using a homemade herbal shampoo or rinse as a natural and gentle substitute for a commercially produced product.

Soapwort (*Saponaria officinalis*) is an interesting herb which gained its name from the fact that it works as a gentle shampoo or cleanser for hair and textiles. The roots and leaves of soapwort are used to produce a liquid which lathers, and removes grease and dirt. Soapwort has been used since Roman times and probably even earlier. It is possible to buy the plant dried to use in making natural shampoos.

Elderflower Rinse

*R*insing the hair and removing every trace of shampoo is an important part of achieving shiny and truly clean hair. This basic recipe for a rinse could be made with chamomile instead, if you prefer. If used frequently, chamomile will have a gentle and slight, but progressive, bleaching effect on mousey or blonde hair. Keep a bottle of this liquid in the bathroom and pour some over the hair as the very last rinse.

2 quarts water
2 handfuls dried elderflowers or
4 handfuls of fresh flowers
1 lemon

2 Boil the water and pour it over the elderflowers in the bowl. Stir it thoroughly and leave to infuse until cold. Squeeze the juice of the lemon and strain it.

1 Gather your ingredients together. Place the flowers in a large bowl.

3 Strain the liquid and discard the elderflowers. Add the strained lemon juice, and mix well. Pour into bottles and cork securely. Use a cupful or so as a final rinse.

Soapwort and Egg Shampoo

*T*his is mild and gentle and excellent for any hair type. Be sure to rinse out every trace.

1 cup water
1 tbsp dried soapwort
1 egg yolk
Juice of one lemon, strained

Boil the water and pour it over the soapwort. Stir well, then leave to infuse, and cool. Whisk the egg yolk and strained lemon juice together, and add to the cooled soapwort infusion. Store in the refrigerator.

Box and Bay Hair Tonic

*T*his robust tonic is designed for men. It should strengthen the hair and stimulate the scalp. It can be used as a rinse, or simply brushed through the hair between washes. Use fresh boxwood leaves and bay if you can; it may be hard to find dried box. If you cannot get hold of box, then substitute dried yarrow or fennel to go with the bay leaves. You will need:

1 cup bay leaves
1 cup boxwood leaves
2 quarts water
²⁄₃ cup eau-de-cologne
²⁄₃ cup cider vinegar

Box

1 Gather together and measure
out all the ingredients you require.
Select a bottle that can be made
airtight for storing the tonic.

2 *Strip off the leaves and put them into a pan. Add water, and bring to the boil. Simmer 20 minutes. Leave to cool.*

3 *Strain the liquid from the leaves, which you should discard. Add the eau-de-cologne to the vinegar, and then pour this mixture into the herb mixture. Bottle. Shake well each time before using.*

Sage and Rosemary Rinse

*T*his rinse is meant for brunettes. Used often, it adds luster and depth to dark hair color. Fresh herbs are pleasant to use, but you can also use dried ones. Make it in the same way as the elder-flower rinse, but use ½ cup cider vinegar in place of the lemon juice and a handful of each of the herbs, or two handfuls each if they are fresh. Rosemary is supposed to help prevent dandruff and other scalp problems. It is slightly antiseptic.

Herbal Information

HARVESTING AND
PRESERVING HERBS
Pages 204-207

A REFERENCE GUIDE
TO HERBS
Pages 208-215

HERB SOURCES
Pages 216-217

INDEX
Pages 218-219

CREDITS
Pages 220

Harvesting and Preserving Herbs

Fresh herb leaves and flowers add flavor and color to salads and a variety of other dishes, as well as beauty and fragrance to the home in the form of decorations and arrangements. Although it is usually preferable to use fresh rather than dried herbs in cooking, in order to reap the full benefits, this is often only possible at certain seasons of the year. In the past, before the days of modern farming techniques and imported fruits and vegetables, one of the few ways in which the flavor of summer could be preserved for the coming winter months was by drying herbs, and this is still the next best option to using fresh ones. Dried herb flowers and foliage may not be comparable to the fresh plants, but they are pretty and decorative in their own, different way, and can be used to create long-lasting displays and decorations. When infused, some dried herbs release their aromatic flavors to make delicious and therapeutic teas and tisanes, while other highly scented, dried herbs can be used in potpourris or to fill sachets for perfuming clothes in storage. Dried herbs can also be used in bath and beauty preparations, and in smaller quantities than fresh herbs.

Herbs that dry well and retain their flavor, fragrance, and potency are those that grow as fairly shrubby plants, such as rosemary, thyme, bay, sage, and marjoram. Other herbs can be dried, but lose the fullness of their flavor and aroma in the process, so larger quantities of the dried herb should be used in recipes. These include parsley, mint, tarragon, chervil, fennel, and dill. Some of the more delicate herb plants, including chives, borage, basil, and balm, are rather less successful when dried, so use them fresh whenever possible.

If you plan to use herb leaves, these should be harvested just as the plants come into flower, and before the seeds form. Gather the herbs in the morning as soon as the dew has evaporated and before the warmth of the sun has begun to draw out the oils that give them their flavor and aroma; they begin to wilt in the heat of the day. Discard any old or discolored leaves, or any that have been damaged by insects. This is especially important if you are going to use the leaves for decoration, as the appearance will be spoiled.

Herb flowers for display are best harvested at midday in dry weather. Cut the stems just before the flowers are about to open fully. Pick them carefully to avoid damaging the petals.

Herbs need to be dried as quickly as possible in order to preserve their flavor and color. However, drying them in direct sunlight will damage them. They can be dried in several different ways. Individual leaves and flowers can be placed on trays covered with absorbent paper towel or on wire cake racks, and left in a warm, dry, dark place, such as a heated basement or in a very shady part of a porch. Alternatively,

Lovage

RIGHT: *Sprigs of dried bay are excellent for use in displays but for cooking it is better to use the fresh leaves.*

BELOW: *Many herbs retain their flavor and fragrance well when dried. In a few cases, the potency is enhanced through drying.*

Fennel

heat the oven on its lowest setting, or with only the pilot light on, and place the herbs inside to dry. Check regularly to make sure they do not burn.

A pretty and traditional way to dry whole stems of herbs, especially flowering and decorative herbs for display, is to air-dry them. Strip the lower leaves from the stems and group them into bunches. Tie the stems together with a long length of string and hang the bunches upside down in a warm, dry, dark place to dry. Do not leave the bunches there indefinitely, though, as the herbs can become dusty and lose their flavor and fragrance after some time.

One of the quickest ways to dry herb leaves is to use the microwave oven. Herb flowers are not as easily dried in this way. Strip the leaves from the stems and place them in a single layer on a sheet of absorbent paper towel. Cook on HIGH for 30 seconds, then turn the leaves over and cook for a further 30 seconds to 1 minute, checking at 5-second intervals to be sure the leaves don't burn. A note of caution - older-model microwaves can be damaged by this process. Consult your machine's instructions or manufacturer before attempting to use it to dry herbs.

To store the dried herb leaves, strip them from their stalks if necessary and put them into Mason jars or cloth bags. Label the jars carefully – herbs tend to look similar when dried, and it is easy to forget which is which. Store them in a dark place.

To help preserve their flavor, do not crumble the leaves of culinary herbs until just before you want to use them.

The color and shape of individual flowers is best preserved by using silica gel crystals, but only for decorative purposes. Roses are particularly suitable for this treatment. Place a 1 inch layer of dry silica gel crystals in an airtight container, then carefully arrange the flower heads over it. Spoon further crystals over the flowers until they are completely covered. Cover the container with a tight-fitting lid and leave in a warm, dry place for two to three days. Remove the flowers carefully as they will be brittle.

Dried herb seeds, such as coriander, dill, and aniseed often have a quite distinctive, spicy flavor, and may be an important ingredient in certain dishes, including relishes and drinks. Caraway seeds and poppyseeds are used to flavor and decorate cakes and breads. To dry the seeds, cut the seedheads from the plant just as they begin to turn brown. Place in large paper bags and leave to dry in a warm room. As the seeds dry, they will fall to the bottom of the paper bag. Store the seeds in Mason jars away from direct light.

Fresh herbs can also be frozen, although the majority of herbs become rather limp when thawed. The most suitable

RIGHT: Herbs tied into bunches with pretty ribbons and hung up in the kitchen to air-dry make a really pleasing display.

Dill

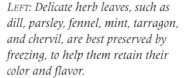

LEFT: Delicate herb leaves, such as dill, parsley, fennel, mint, tarragon, and chervil, are best preserved by freezing, to help them retain their color and flavor.

herbs for this method are those such as parsley, dill, and fennel, which tend to lose some of their flavor when dried. Wash the herbs and dry them thoroughly. Tie them in small bunches and place them in small plastic freezer bags. Seal the bags to make them airtight and place them in the freezer. When required, the frozen bunches of herbs can be added directly to stews and soups. Herbs such as parsley can even be crumbled while still frozen.

An attractive way to freeze small portions of herbs is to freeze them in ice cubes. They make a particularly attractive and unusual garnish for long summer drinks, such as punches and coolers. Suitable herbs include mint and salad burnet leaves and colorful borage flowers, all of which will give a subtle flavor to the drink. Simply place the herbs in an ice-cube tray and fill with water, then place in the freezer as usual. Use mineral water or spring water for the best effect, as tap water tends to go cloudy when frozen.

Another way to preserve the flavors of fresh herbs is to use them to make herb vinegars that can be added to salad dressings and sauces. Suitable herbs are tarragon, basil, and garlic (see page 78). Herb flowers such as marigold, elderflower, and chives can also be preserved by steeping them in vinegar in this way, giving a more delicate flavor to the liquid. These vinegars look attractive on display in the kitchen.

Herbs can be preserved in coarse (kosher) salt, and this method is useful for herbs that do not dry well, such as basil. Starting with a layer of salt at the bottom of an airtight jar, add alternate layers of salt and leaves, finishing with a final layer of salt. Shake or rinse the leaves when you use them.

Herb butters are an easy and attractive way of using herbs in cooking. Simply chop the herbs and beat them into butter with a little seasoning and lemon juice. Parsley, chervil, chives, and tarragon are suitable, or use a mixture of herbs. The butter can be placed in ice-cube trays in the freezer, then used as a garnish for snacks and vegetables, steaks and barbecued meats, releasing the flavor of the herbs as it melts.

The flowers, leaves, and stems of some herbs can be candied, making them decorative and tasty additions to cakes and desserts. Dainty violet flowers retain both their color and taste when prepared in this way. To candy violets, simply coat the flowers lightly with beaten egg white, then dip them into superfine sugar. Dry them gently in a slow oven, or leave them near the heater in the basement between layers of wax or parchment paper. When they are completely dry store them in an airtight container. Rose petals and borage flowers can also be preserved using this method, as can mint and scented geranium leaves.

Angelica stalks can be candied and used to decorate cakes and creamy desserts. These delicious sweetmeats take on a characteristic bright green color when boiled in syrup with green leaves (see page 79). Store in an airtight container.

A Reference Guide to Herbs

Allium sativum
GARLIC

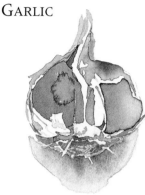

Garlic has thin, bright green leaves which grow from the sheath of a slender cylindrical stem. It grows to a height of about 12 inches, and its globe-shaped flower head contains small white florets. Garlic is a hardy perennial and grows from a bulb which is divided up into cloves. The distinctive flavor of the bulb is used widely in cooking. Garlic prefers a well-drained, rich, moist soil in a sunny position

Allium schoenoprasum
CHIVES

Chives grow in clumps up to 6–10 inches high with bright

green, thin, cylindrical stems topped with large pink or mauve pompom flowers in midsummer. Often used for garnishing food, their delicate oniony flavor is used in salads and soft cheeses, and the flowers add color to herb vinegars. Chives prefer a rich, damp soil and should be grown in a sunny position, but they need plenty of water.

Aloysia triphylla
LEMON VERBENA, HERB LOUISA

Lemon verbena is a fragrant, perennial shrub which produces masses of pale purple or white flowers. Its slender leaves smell strongly of lemon, and they can be used fresh in fruit salads, punches, and coolers, or dried and added to potpourris and bath preparations. Lemon verbena is not hardy and must be overwintered indoors in most of the U.S.

Anethum graveolens
DILL

Dill is a fragrant hardy annual with fine, feathery green leaves and small, deep-yellow flowers

growing in flat heads. The plant will grow to a height of 2–3 feet. The leaves are often used in savory sauces to accompany fish, or chopped and added to salads. The seeds can be used in stews, soups, vinegars, and relishes. Dill prefers to grow in a sunny position and fine, well-drained soil.

Angelica archangelica
ANGELICA

Angelica is a large biennial herb with glossy green leaves and self-seeding white flowers. It is a hardy plant which can grow to a height of 3-6 feet. Angelica is best known for its candied form. The bright green stems are used to decorate cakes, but its sweet leaves can also be used to flavor preserves or fruit dishes. Angelica thrives in wetter climates, growing well in rich soil and partially shaded areas.

Anthriscus cerefolium
CHERVIL

Chervil is a fern-like annual and grows to a height of about 18 inches. It has pale green leaves and small white flowers, and both flat and curly-leaved varieties are available. Combined with parsley, tarragon, and thyme, chervil is one of the classic *fine herbes* used in French cooking. It has a subtle aniseed flavor and can be used in salads and soups. Chervil prefers a well-drained, partially shady site.

Artemisia abrotanum
SOUTHERNWOOD, FIELD SOUTHERNWOOD, ARTEMISIA

Southernwood is a woody perennial with gray-green

feathery leaves which, when crushed, have a lemon scent. The plant sometimes produces small yellow flowers and will grow to a height of 3 feet if cut back. When dried, the leaves can be added to linen sachets as they will repel moths and other insects. Good for growing in containers, southernwood thrives in light, well-drained soil in a sunny position.

Artemisia dracunculus
TARRAGON, FRENCH TARRAGON

Tarragon is a bushy, perennial herb with slender, aromatic green leaves. The plant produces small white flowers in late summer and can grow to a height of 3 feet. Fresh tarragon can be added to salads and vegetable dishes and used to flavor mayonnaise, preserves, vinegars, and liqueurs. Tarragon prefers good, well-drained soil and a sunny position. It also grows well in pots and containers.

Borage officinalis
BORAGE

One of the prettiest herbs to grow, Borage has abundant sky blue or pink star-shaped flowers

with distinctive black centers. The flowers and leaves may be used to flavor liqueurs, to decorate summer drinks, and to add color to fresh herb posies. Borage is an annual herb and grows quickly from seed to become a large, sprawling plant, reaching a height of 18–30 inches. It will thrive in a poor chalky or sandy soil with plenty of sun.

Buxus sempervirens
BOX

Box is an evergreen tree with dense, small, dark green, glossy leaves. It is slow-growing but can reach a height of 15–20 feet, though it is often used for low hedging and for decorative topiary. Box is not hardy in zones colder than 5. The leaves and branches are attractive in floral and herbal decorations, and the leaves can also be used to make a hair tonic. It prefers a well-drained soil.

Calendula officinalis
MARIGOLD

Marigold is a popular hardy annual grown from seed and its brightly colored orange or

yellow flowers add cheer to any garden. The fresh flowers can be scattered over salads and dried flowers added to potpourri to give vibrant color.

Marigold helps to soften calloused skin and is used in beauty preparations. It will thrive in a sunny position and prefers a moist, rich soil. Dead-head the plants frequently to encourage new flowers.

Carum carvi
CARAWAY

Caraway is a biennial plant with a slender, pale green, furrowed stem and feathery leaves. Its delicate flower heads bear tiny white florets and the plant grows to a height of 1½–2 feet. The aromatic seeds are used to flavor cakes and breads and may also be added to a variety of meat dishes. Caraway prefers a well-drained, light soil and a sunny position.

Thuja occidentalis
CEDARWOOD, YELLOW CEDAR

This conifer is the tallest of this species of cedar tree and can grow to a height of 30 feet. Its pungent aroma is similar to that of balsam and acts as an insect repellent, so the wood has traditionally been used to make closets and chests. Cedarwood shavings can be used to make scented sachets and potpourris, while the essential oil is used to impregnate wooden shapes.

Chamaemelum nobile
CHAMOMILE, CAMOMILE

Chamomile is an annual herb with small, scented yellow-and-white flowers. It has a great many healing and cosmetic uses. Fresh or dried leaves make a soothing tea to settle indigestion, and a simple infusion of chamomile flowers makes a good herbal rinse for fair hair. Chamomile is very easy to grow from seeds sown in early spring, preferring a dry, sunny position and light, well-drained soil.

Coriandrum sativum
CORIANDER, CILANTRO

Coriander is an easy-to-grow hardy annual. Its lower leaves are bright green and look similar to flat-leaved parsley, while the upper leaves are feathery. The plant grows to a height of 2 feet and has small, pinkish white flowers. The aromatic seeds are used to flavor foods, while the leaves have a sharp taste and can be added to salads and vegetable dishes. Coriander prefers a light, rich soil and a sunny position.

Crataegus monogyna
HAWTHORN, MAY, MAY BLOSSOM

The thorny deciduous hawthorn tree can grow to a height of 23 feet. It has mid-green, lobed leaves and bears white flowers in late spring, followed by red berries or "haws" in early fall. The freshly picked blossom can be used to flavor brandy and liqueurs. A fast-growing tree, hawthorn prefers a sunny, open position and is often used as decorative hedging.

Dianthus sp.
PINK, CLOVE PINK

There are several *Dianthus* species. They have long, thin leaves and jointed stems. The attractive scented flowers have serrated petals, sometimes picotee-edged, in a wide range of colors. The flowers can be used fresh in flower arrangements and posies or dried for use in potpourris. They can also be used to flavor and decorate salads, and to flavor sugar, vinegars, and wine. *Dianthus* prefers a well-drained soil and an open, sunny position.

Eucalyptus globulus
EUCALYPTUS

Eucalyptus is an evergreen tree with gray-green leaves. It is an easy-to-grow tree and can reach a height of 300 feet. The rounded leaves of the juvenile tree are used in flower arrangements and garlands, and the dried leaves may be added to give color and fragrance to

potpourris. Eucalyptus may be used in foot treatments as it peps up the circulation. Oil is extracted from the leaves for medicinal use.

Foeniculum vulgare
FENNEL

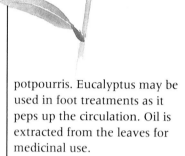

Fennel is a hardy perennial with aromatic, feathery leaves which can be either green or bronze in color. From midsummer, the plant produces bright yellow flowers. The leaves and seeds can be used to give a sweet aniseed flavor to food. Its health-giving properties are of use in skin and hair preparations. Fennel grows to a height of 5–6 feet and prefers a well-drained soil and plenty of sun.

Gallium odoratum
SWEET WOODRUFF

Woodruff has delicate white flowers which bloom in early summer and narrow leaves which grow in star-shaped ruff formations. It is a low-growing plant, rarely reaching more than 8 inches in height. Its dried leaves have the sweet smell of new-mown hay, making it an attractive addition to bath gel and herb bags. The flowers are used to flavor summer drinks. Woodruff grows well in moist, rich soil in partial shade.

Humulus lupulus
HOP

The hop is a perennial vine. It produces yellowish green female "cones" which contain flowers and embryonic fruits. When dried, these parts of the plant are used to flavor beer. The young shoots and immature leaves can be added to vegetable soups or cooked on their own. Hops have a slightly sedative effect and the dried flowers are a traditional ingredient in herbal sleep pillows. Hops need plenty of sun and a rich soil to thrive.

Hyssopus officinalis
HYSSOP

Hyssop has aromatic, dark green leaves and woody stems, and during its long growing season produces pink, blue, and white flowers. An evergreen perennial, it grows to a height of 1–2 feet. Hyssop has a strong, minty taste and smell, and can be used fresh or dried in herbal insect repellents, posies, and potpourris. It prefers a sunny position and well-drained soil.

Jasminum sp.
JASMINE

There are many forms of Jasmine, some evergreen, and most are climbing plants. The summer-flowering *Jasminum officinale* bears small, white, sweetly scented blossoms, while the winter-flowering *Jasminum nudiflorum* has yellow flowers. Jasmine is not hardy (tropical or subtropical). The flowers are used to make scent sachets and potpourris. Oil extracted from jasmine can also be used to scent candles. *Jasminum sambac* is the variety used to scent tea. Small varieties are available to be grown as pot-plants.

Juglans regia
WALNUT, ENGLISH WALNUT

The walnut is a deciduous tree with a wide-spreading crown of large, bright green, oval-shaped leaves. It can grow to a height of 30 feet. The tree's ripe nuts can be eaten on their own or added to cakes and sauces, while the green nuts can be pickled in vinegar. Their skins are used to make a rinse for dark hair and walnut leaves are used in a soothing footbath. Walnut prefers a well-drained, chalky soil.

Laurus nobilis
BAY, LAUREL, SWEET BAY

Bay is an evergreen tree with glossy green leaves and small, creamy white flowers. Hardy only to zone 7, it must be overwintered indoors in most of the U.S. Although slow growing, it can grow up to 26 feet. Bay leaves are one of the herbs used in *bouquet garni*. Bay can also be used fresh or dried in beauty preparations and in arrangements and potpourris. Bay prefers a sheltered, sunny position and rich, well-drained soil.

Lavandula angustifolia
LAVENDER

There are many varieties of lavender, ranging from dark purple to mauve, pink, and white. A hardy, evergreen shrub, it grows as a compact bush up to 30 inches in height. The clean smell of lavender is a traditional fragrance with a wide range of cosmetic and decorative uses in sachets, bath preparations, and skin lotions. Lavender will thrive in poor but well-drained soil in a sunny position.

Melissa officinalis
LEMON BALM, MELISSA

Lemon balm, a member of the mint family, is a perennial. Its pale green or variegated leaves both taste and smell of lemon.

It grows to a height of 2-3 feet and produces pale yellow or white flowers throughout the summer. Fresh lemon balm leaves make a refreshing tea, served hot or cold, and they enhance the flavor of lemonade and herb jellies. The plant prefers poor, moist soil and a sunny position.

Mentha sp.
MINT

There are many varieties of mint. It is used for many culinary and medicinal purposes. Fresh or dried leaves make a refreshing tea, and mint is traditionally used in mint julep. In England, it flavors sauces and jellies accompanying lamb. Beauty treatments based on mint cool the skin. Mint prefers to grow in moist, well-drained soil in partial shade or sun.

Mentha piperata
PEPPERMINT

Peppermint has the strongest flavor of all the mint varieties. It is widely grown commercially for many medicinal and cosmetic uses, such as toothpaste. The leaves make a refreshing herbal tea, and dried leaves keep their flavor well. Peppermint tones up the circulation and makes a good treatment for tired or swollen feet. It is one of the most important essential oils. Peppermint thrives in a fairly warm, moist climate and prefers open textured, well-drained soils.

Mentha pulegium
PENNYROYAL, RUN-BY-THE-GROUND, LURK-IN-THE-DITCH

Pennyroyal is quite unlike other varieties of the mint family. Rather than producing a bushy plant, it grows as a low-lying, creeping half-hardy perennial, making it ideal ground cover. Pennyroyal should not be used in cooking since it can be toxic. It is traditionally regarded as a flea repellent, and the fresh leaves may be rubbed into a pet's coat as a remedy. The dried leaves can be used in potpourris. It will grow in any type of soil but prefers moist conditions, in partial shade or sun.

Mentha suaveolens rotundifolia
APPLEMINT

Applemint has less invasive growing habits than other varieties of mint. The rounded leaves have an apple fragrance and its milder, sweeter taste makes it ideal for use in cakes, and in dishes and drinks using fruit. The dried leaves retain their fragrance well and fresh sprigs look attractive in aromatic herb posies. Applemint can grow to a height of 2 feet and thrives in rich, moist soil and partial shade.

Monarda didyma
BERGAMOT, OSWEGO, BEE BALM

Bergamot is a fragrant perennial herb with distinctive,

bright red flowers which attract bees. It can grow to a height of 18–36 inches. The dried leaves can be infused as a tea, and oil of bergamot used to scent candles and colognes. Care should be taken, however, as skin reactions can occur in some people. Bergamot prefers a rich, moist soil and partial shade, and needs to be kept well watered.

Ocimum basilicum
BASIL

Growing to a height of 1–2 feet, basil has large shiny leaves and small white flowers. It is best known for its culinary uses, especially with tomatoes and as the basis for pesto sauce. Basil is one of the few herbs that does not dry well, so use fresh leaves if possible. Young leaves are the sweetest, so it is best to sow plenty of seeds to ensure a constant crop and remove the flowers to encourage leaf growth. If using dried leaves, pulverize them to release the full aroma. An annual, basil thrives in a sunny position and

light, rich soil, but be careful not to over-water.

Ocimum basilicum 'Purpurescens'
PURPLE BASIL

This attractive variety of basil is suitable to grow in pots and useful to add color to salads and vinegars.

Origanum onites
MARJORAM, POT MARJORAM, FRENCH MARJORAM

Marjoram is a sweetly scented herb often used in Mediterranean cookery. It grows as a small bush with tiny green leaves and pink flowers.

Fresh or dried leaves give flavor to salads and jellies as well as meat dishes, and the flowers make attractive additions to decorative arrangements. Marjoram can be air-dried in bunches and keeps its flavor and aroma well. Use it in dried herb sachets to scent clothes and repel insects. Marjoram can be grown from seed in the spring and prefers a rich, well-drained soil. It can be grown in pots on its own or in tubs and window-boxes with other compact herbs. It is not hardy and must be overwintered indoors.

Origanum vulgare 'Aureum'
GOLDEN MARJORAM

This variety of marjoram has golden-colored leaves that will scorch in full sun, and a mild flavor. Its attractive color makes it especially suitable for making decorative garlands and wreaths from the fresh herbs.

Papaver somniferum
POPPY

This annual poppy has gray-green leaves and distinctive large flowers with papery petals in a wide range of colors from white to dark pink. There are also double-flowered forms similar to peonies and

carnations. It freely self-seeds in the garden, so that once established, plants reappear each year. The dried seed-heads make an attractive addition to floral arrangements. Poppies prefer a well-drained soil in full sun.

Pelargonium sp.
GERANIUM, PELARGONIUM

Commonly called geraniums, there are many scented-leaved pelargoniums in a range of white, pinks, and reds. They are evergreen perennials but are tender plants and are usually grown in containers so that

they can be moved inside. The leaves, with their scents of rose, apple, peppermint, orange, lemon, and cinnamon, can be used fresh or dried in potpourris. Oil is extracted for use in beauty preparations. The leaves are also used in salads, and frosted to decorate cakes.

Petroselinum crispum
PARSLEY

Parsley is one of the most popular culinary herbs. It is a biennial, so the leaves should be used in its first year, before it goes to seed the following year. There are two varieties – curly-leaved and flat-leaved. The plant ranges in height from dwarf types suitable for growing in pots to varieties which can reach 2 feet. Most of the flavor is in the stalks. Parsley is used for sauces, soups, and salads. The curly-leaved variety is most often used for garnishing. Parsley prefers a sunny position and rich, moist soil.

Rosa sp.
ROSE

The fragrant rose has been used for centuries for medicinal, culinary, and cosmetic purposes. Fresh and dried buds, flower heads, and petals are

used for their color and scent in potpourris, scent sachets, and skin preparations. Oil is also extracted from the flowers. The damask rose and cabbage rose are the main species used for aromatherapy. Petals are also used for teas, jams, vinegars, and wines. Roses prefer a well-drained soil in an open, sunny or partially shaded position.

Rosmarinus officinalis
ROSEMARY

Rosemary is a strong-flavored, hardy, evergreen herb. It has aromatic, needle-shaped, blue-green leaves. In late spring and during mild weather it produces blue, pink, or white flowers. Rosemary has many uses as a flavoring in food and liqueurs and in decorative arrangements, potpourris, and beauty treatments. When dried, the leaves keep their flavor well. This herb grows best in light, dry soil and a sheltered position. It is more fragrant if grown on a chalky soil. It is hardy only to zone 6.

Rumex acetosa
SORREL, BROAD-LEAVED SORREL

Sorrel is similar to spinach in appearance and taste and should be cooked in the same way. It will grow to 2 feet in height, producing reddish green flowers in midsummer. A perennial, sorrel should be kept cut back to enable the harvest of tender leaves through the season. It is often used to flavor mayonnaise and sauce to accompany fish, in tarts and soups, and the young leaves can be eaten raw in salads. In spring the leaves are tasteless, but develop in acidity as the season progresses. Sorrel will grow in most types of soil.

Rumex scutatus
BUCKLER-SHAPED SORREL, FRENCH SORREL

This variety of sorrel has a slightly milder flavor than Broad-leaved sorrel. Its attractive leaves make it suitable for growing in window-boxes with a selection of other culinary herbs.

Salvia officinalis
SAGE

There are many varieties of green sage, of which Garden sage is the most common. It is a strongly-flavored, aromatic, hardy shrub which can grow to a height of 4 feet. It is only evergreen outside the cold-winter areas of the U.S. Other varieties include Golden sage, Pineapple sage and Red or Purple sage. Sage leaves are used both fresh and dried for culinary, decorative, and aromatic purposes. Sage will grow in any well-drained soil in a sunny position.

Sambucus nigra
ELDERFLOWER

Elder is a hardy deciduous shrub or tree. There are two varieties – the European elder grows to a height of 22 feet, while the smaller, shrubbier American variety reaches a height of 12 feet. Its creamy white flowers bloom in early summer and produce a lovely scent. They are used for skin and hair preparations and for

vinegars, wines, and cordials. The berries can be made into wine or used in jam-making.

Santolina chamaecyparissus
SANTOLINA, COTTON LAVENDER

Santolina is a hardy but not evergreen shrub with aromatic silver-green, feathery leaves and small, yellow, button flowers. Often planted as hedging, santolina grows to a height of 2 feet. Its leaves and flowers may be used fresh in decorative arrangements or dried in scent sachets and potpourris. The pungent scent repels moths and insects. Santolina prefers a sandy, well-drained soil in an open sunny position.

Saponaria officinalis
SOAPWORT, BOUNCING BET, SOAPROOT, WILD SWEET WILLIAM

Soapwort is an attractive herb with large, pale pink flowers. It usually reaches to a height of 2 feet, but can grow to 5 feet. This herb is not scented but the leaves and root macerated in water produce a gentle lather

excellent for cleaning delicate fabrics. Dried soapwort can be used to make hair shampoo. It thrives in a sunny position and moist soil.

Symphytum officinale
COMFREY

Comfrey is a member of the borage family. It is a hardy perennial with long, coarse gray-green leaves, and produces blue or cream flowers throughout the summer. A tall, spreading plant which grows to a height of 2–3 feet, it seeds itself. Traditionally used in poultices to alleviate bruising, comfrey can be added to herbal bath gel. Comfrey will grow in almost any type of well-drained, fertile soil.

Tanacetum parthenium
FEVERFEW, FLIRTWORT, BACHELOR'S BUTTONS

Feverfew has lacy yellow or green leaves and distinctive, daisy-like, yellow-and-white flowers. The aromatic leaves are not often used in cooking due to their bitter taste, but they have been proved to be effective in curing headaches. The flowers make colorful decorations in fresh herbal arrangements. A hardy perennial, the plant reaches a height of 18–24 inches and thrives in a well-drained, moist soil and full sunlight.

Tanacetum vulgare
TANSY, BUTTONS

Tansy is a hardy perennial with aromatic green leaves and clusters of yellow flowers. It is one of the taller herbs, reaching a height of 3–4 feet. Tansy is grown mainly for decorative purposes and may also be used as a herbal insect repellant in sachets. Tansy will thrive in most types of soil.

Thymus citriodorus
LEMON THYME

This variety of thyme is sweetly scented. Its small, bright green leaves have a mild citrus flavor. An evergreen herb, it grows to a height of 8–12 inches and produces dark pink flowers in late summer. It is a popular culinary herb for poultry and stuffings, and can also be used to flavor jellies and ice cream. Lemon thyme prefers a dry, well-drained soil.

Thymus vulgaris
THYME, COMMON THYME, GARDEN THYME

There are many varieties of thyme and Common thyme is a cultivated form of the wild herb. This aromatic variety is a spreading evergreen perennial which grows to a maximum height of about 9 inches and produces small mauve flowers in summer. Thyme is a

traditional ingredient of *bouquet garni*. It is also used fresh or dried as a flavoring in jellies and vinegars, and decoratively in potpourris, wreaths, and garlands. Thyme prefers a sunny position and will grow in any well-drained soil.

Tilia × vulgaris
LIME, LINDEN BLOSSOM

The lime or linden is a deciduous tree with glossy green, heart-shaped leaves. It grows to a height of 50 feet and produces heavily scented yellow flowers. When picked young, the dried blossom can be used to make a popular relaxing herbal tea. The dried flowers and linden oil can also be used in potpourris. The lime tree prefers a well-drained soil in a sunny position.

Vanilla planifolia
VANILLA

The vanilla is a tender climbing plant of the orchid family that grows in tropical conditions, reaching a height of 40 feet. It has long, leathery leaves and produces yellow or orange flowers. The flowers are followed by long, aromatic fruit pods called beans which, when dried, can be used to flavor a wide variety of foodstuffs from ice cream to cakes and candy. Vanilla oil is also used in perfumes, potpourris, and scented candles.

Viola odorata
VIOLET, SWEET VIOLET

Violet is a small perennial with heart-shaped leaves and dainty sweet scented violet or white flowers. An oil can be extracted from the flowers and the flowers used to flavor liqueurs, vinegars, and candy. They may also be used in posies and potpourris. When candied or frosted, the flowers make an attractive decoration for cakes and fruit salads. Violet prefers a humus-rich soil and semi-shade.

Zingiber officinale
GINGER

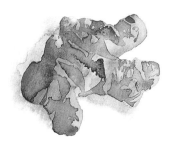

Ginger is a tender creeping plant that grows in tropical conditions, reaching a height of 3–4 feet. It has reed-like stems with lance-shaped leaves which grow from rhizomes or roots. The roots may be used fresh in sauces and oriental dishes, or ground to provide a warming, spicy flavor in cakes, cookies, beers, ales, and wine. When ground, ginger can be used to scent pomanders and potpourris. Ginger requires a rich soil and a tropical climate.

Herb Sources

Fresh Herbs

Le Jardin du Gourmet
P.O. Box 75
St. Johnsbury Center, VT 05863
802/748-1446

Mellinger's, Inc.
2310 West South Range Road
North Lima, OH 44452
216/549-9861
Orders: 800/321-7444

Companion's Plants
7247 North Coolville Ridge
Athens, OH 45701
614/592-4643
800/529-3344

Goodwin Creek Gardens
Box 83
Williams, OR 97544
503/846-7357

Sandy Mush Herb Nursery
316 Surrett Cove Road
Leicester, NC 28748-9622
704/683-2014
Catalog: $4

Rabbit Shadow Farm
2880 Highway 402
Loveland, CO 80537
303/667-5531
Orders: 800/850-5531
Fax: 303/667-0616

Edgewood Gardens
2611 Corrine Drive
Orlando, FL 32803
407/896-3203

Loggee's Greenhouses
141 North Street
Danielson, CN 06239
Catalog: $3

Tinmouth Channel Farm
Box 428B-HCD
Tinmouth, VT 05773
Catalog: $2

Patinsky Farm
902 Foster Street
South Windsor, CT 06074
203/644-4268

Little Farm Herb Shop
146 West Chicago Road
Allen, MI 49227

Brown's Edgewood Gardens
2611 Corrine Drive
Orlando, FL 32803
407/896-3203
Catalog: $2

Vineyard Sound Herbs
RFD 900
Vineyard Haven, MA 02568
508/696-7574
Catalog: $1
517/869-2822

Lily of the Valley Herb Farm
3969 Fox Avenue
Minerva, OH 44657
216/862-3920
Plant & seed list: $1
Product list: $1

Nichols Garden Nursery
1190 South Pacific
Albany, OR 97321
503/928-9280

The Thyme Garden
20546-H Alsea Highway
Alsea, OR 97324
503/487-8671
Catalog: $1.50

Edgewood Farm & Nursery
Route 2, Box 303
Stanardsville, VA 22973-9405
804/985-3782
Catalog: $2

Wrenwood
Route 4, Box 361
Berkeley Springs, WV 25411
304/258-3071

Herbs-Liscious
1702 South Sixth Street
Marshalltown, IA 50158
Catalog: $2

Renaissance Acres
4450 Valentine
Whitmore Lake, MI 48189

Aimer Seeds
81 Temperance Street
Aurora
Ontario L4G 2R1
905/841-6226

Country Lane Herbs
RR3
Puslinch
Ontario N0B 2J0 Canada
905/659-7327

Cruickshank's
1015 Mount Pleasant Road
Toronto
Ontario M4P 2M1 Canada
416/488-8292

Lowland Herb Farm
5685 Lickman Road
RR 3 Sardis
British Columbia V0X 1Y0
604/858-4216 Canada

McFayden Seeds
30 Ninth Street, Suite 200
Brandon
Manitoba R7A 6N4 Canada
800/205-7111

McConnell Nurseries
Port Burwell
Ontario N0J 1T0 Canada
800/363-0901

Richters Herbs
357 Highway 47
Goodwood
Ontario L0C 1A0 Canada
905/640-6677

Stokes Seeds
39 James Street, Box 10
St. Catherines
Ontario L2R 6R6 Canada
905/688-4300

Stokes Seeds
Box 548
Buffalo, NY 14240-0548
716/695-6980

Thompson & Morgan
P.O. Box 1308, Dept. PR5
Jackson, NJ 08527
US: 800/274-7333
Can: 908/363-2225

Vessey Seeds, Ltd.
York
Prince Edward Island C0A 1P0
Canada
Orders: 902/368-7333
Fax: 902/566-1620

William Dam Seeds Ltd.
Box 8400
Dundas
Ontario L9H 6M1 Canada
905/628-6641

Fresh and Dried Herbs

Mountain Rose Herbs
P.O. Box 2000 H
Redway, CA 95560
707/923-3941

Braeloch Farm
9124 North 35th
Richaland, MI 49083
616/629-9884

Fresh Herbs and Dried Flowers

Rasland Farm
Route 1, Box 65C
Godwin, NC 28344
910/567-2705
Catalog: $2.50

Shady Acres Herb Farm
7815 Highway 212
Chaska, MN 55318
Voice/fax: 612/466-3991

Well-Sweep Herb Farm
317 Mt. Bethel Road
Port Murray, NJ 07865
908/852-5390

Meadowsweet Herb Farm
729D Mt. Holly Road
North Shrewsbury, VT 05738
802/492-3565

Gilbertie's Herb Gardens
7 Sylvan Lane
Westport, CT 06880
203/227-4175

Dried Herbs and Flowers

Farmer Ted's Herbs &
Everlastings
1349 Pine Ridge
Bushkill, PA 18324
717/588-3009

Meadow Everlastings
16464 Shabbona Road
Malta, IL 60150
Catalog: $2

The Ginger Tree
245 Lee Road 122
Opelika, AL 36801
Send SASE (business size) for
prices

Mountain Valley Farms
348 Bowman Road
Hamilton, MT 59840
800/225-2543

Tom Thumb Workshops
Mappsville, VA 23407-0357
Catalog: $1
Quarterly newsletter: $15/yr

Hummingbird Farm
2041 N. Zylstra Road
Oak Harbor, WA 98277
206/679-5044
Fax: 800/201-8335

Frontier Cooperative Herbs
3021 Seventh-eighth Street
Norway, IA 52318
319/227-7996

Gardens Past
P.O. Box 1846
Estes Park, CO 80517
Catalog: $1

Premier Botanicals Ltd.
8801 Buena Vista Road
Albany, OR 97321
503/926-5945
Fax: 503/928-2730

Dried Herbs

Capriland Herb Farm
53 Silver Street
Coventry, CT 06238
203/742-7244

Herb 'n' Lore
11 Nadine Court
Thousand Oaks, CA 91320
805/499-7505

Hickory Hill Herbs
307 West Avenue E
Lampasas, TX 76550
512/556-8801

Queen Anne's Herbs
P.O. Box 70105
Eugene, OR 97401
503/687-0166

Fresh and Dried Herbs, Dried Flowers

Lucia's Garden
2942 Virginia Street
Houston, TX 77098
713/523-6494

Windswept Farm
5537 North County Road #9
Fort Collins, CO 80524
303/484-1124

Redding's Country Cabin
Route 1, Box 198-A
Ronda, NC 28670
910/984-4070
Catalog: $2

Country Road Herb Farm and
Gift Barn
1497 Pymatuning Lake Road
Andover, OH 44003
216/577-1932

Candle-Making

The Candle Mill
Old Mill Road
East Arlington, VT 05252
802/375-6068
Orders: 800/772-3759
Free catalog available

Other Resources

The Herb Society of America,
Inc.
9019 Kirtland Chardon Road
Mentor, OH 44060
216/256-0514
Fax: 216/256-0541

The Herb Companion Magazine
201 East 4th Street
Loveland, CO 80537
303/669-7672
$21 for 1 year; $38 for 2 years

International Herb Growers and
Marketers Association
1202 Allanson Road
Mundelein, IL 60060
708/949-4372
Fax: 708/566-4580

Michigan Herb Business
Association
2540 North Setterbo Road
Sutton Bay, MI 49682

Emerson College of Herbology
Ltd.
Dept. A
582 Cummer Avenue
Willowdale, Ontario
Canada M2K 2M4
416/733-2512

Rocky Montain Center for
Botanical Studies
P.O. Box 19254
Boulder, CO 80308-2254
303/442-6861
Catalog: $1

American Horticultural Society
Mt. Vernon, VA
703/768-5700
Call between 11.00 a.m. and
4.00 p.m. EST

There are garden clubs all over
America; for your local branch
contact:
Garden Club of America
598 Madison Avenue
New York, NY 10022
212/753-8287

International Guild of Candle
Artisans
c/o Eleanor Wulff
876 Browning Avenue South
Salem, OR 97302
503/364-5475
Monthly newsletter for
members only. The January
issue is a resource guide with
names and addresses of
mail-order suppliers.
Membership is $25 per year,
and memberships are for the
calendar year. New members
get copies of all the newsletters
already published for the
calendar year. International
memberships welcome.

Index

A

alcohol 178
allspice essential oil *100*
almond & rose hand cream 186-7
angelica *10, 59, 79*, 136, *172*, 208
  cake 59
  candied 59, 79, 207
aniseed 206
applemint *31, 56, 192*, 212
  angel food cake 56
apricot: ice cream 49
  moisturizer 194-5
aromatherapy 94
artemisia *see* southernwood

B

baby's tears in painted pot 151
baking 32-7
baldness 196
ball, red rose 119
balm 204
  footbath 189
barrels 154, *156*
basil *11, 25, 42*, 78, 141, 146,
  149, 204, 207, 212
  in a basket 149
  pesto sauce 42
  purple basil *149*, 212
  roast pepper salad with 25
baskets 121, 149, 157
bath additives 170-5, 204
bay *52*, 104, 112, 124, 132, 160,
  182, 211
  dried 204, *205*
  footbath 189
  hair tonic 200-1
  tree 116-7
beauty preparations 190-5
benzoin, tincture of *182*
bergamot *94, 110, 178*, 212
  essential oil 101, 178
berries 160
borage 204, 206, 207, 209
bouquet garni 72, 112
box 160, *200*, 209
  hair tonic 200-1
  tree, conical 167
boxes, wooden *152-3*, 154-6
brandy 71
breads *33*, 34, 36
bubble bath gel 172-3
bunches/bundles *10*, 130-5
  Christmas tree decorations 164
  insect-repellent 85
  on twig ring 129
  rosemary, marjoram & thyme
    135

butter, herb 207

C

cakes *10*, 52-9, 207
camomile *see* chamomile
candles 217
  decorated 165
  scented 99
candying 79, 207
caraway *32*, 206, 209
  rye bread 36
carnation 78
carrot 192
cassia oil 94
cedarwood *82, 100*, 209
  essential oil 100
chamomile 60, *63*, 104, 184, 186,
  188, 192, 196, 198, 209
  hand gel 188-9
  tisane 63
cheese: & thyme scones 37
  blended with herbs 38
  soft, with herbs *38*, 43-4
  straws, poppyseed 75
chervil *21*, 112, 204, 207, 208
  egg & lemon soup with 20
chili: tortilla chips 35
  wood shaving mixture 96-7
chives *18, 44*, 78, *151, 158*, 204,
  207, 208
  in painted pot 151
  soft cheese with *38*, 43
Christmas decorations 160-7
chutney 74-5
cilantro *see* coriander
cinnamon 130
  with roses 113, 134-5
citrus: herb liqueur 69
  splash 178-9
cleanser, mint 193
colognes 176-83
comfrey 214
containers: pots 136-43
  wooden 152-9
cordials 66-71
coriander *14, 21, 75*, 112, 206,
  210
  chutney with 74-5
  Thai fish soup with 20

D

dill *40*, 204, 206, 208
  & mustard sauce 40
dried herbs 204, 205, 216-7
  displays 111, 113-21, 124,
    160, 204
drinks 60-5

drying: herbs 110, 111, 130,
  204-5
  oranges 96

E

eau de cologne 183
egg: & soapwort shampoo 199
  soup 20-1
elder *70*
elderflower 78, 186, *188*, 192,
  214
  cordial 70
  hand gel 188-9
  rinse 198
emulsions 192
essential oils 82, 94-101, 104,
  114, 170, 173, 176, 184
eucalyptus *104*, 184, 210
  leaf garland 121

F

fennel 184, 192, *195*, 204, *205*,
  206, 210
  bronze fennel 141
feverfew *128*, 215
fish soup with coriander 20-1
fixative 88, 102
fleas 87
flies 82, 87
flowers: harvesting 204
  preserving 206, 207
foam, floral 114, *115*, 124, 126
focaccia, rosemary 34
footbath 189
foot cream 187
fragrances 176-83
freezing herbs 112, 206
frosted geranium leaves 55
fruit: dried 96, 130
  pyramid 162

G

garden containers 136-43,
  152-9
garlands 124-9
garlic *17, 42*, 78, 207, 208
  soft cheese with *38*, 43
  tortilla chips 35
gazpacho with herbs 17
geranium *55*, 104, 144, 146, *151*,
  184, 186, 192, 213
  in box 156
  layer cake 54
  leaves, frosted 55, 207
gifts, edible 72-9
ginger *75*, 215
glue-gun 114

goat's cheese salad 28
golden marjoram *26, 126*, 213
  rose garland 126
growing herbs: indoors 144-51
  outdoors 136-43, 152-9

H

hair rinses 198, 201
hair tonic 200-1
hand cream 186-7
hand gel 188-9
harvesting herbs 204
hawthorn *66*, 210
  may blossom brandy 71
heart, pink rose 118-9
heliotrope 140
hop 210-1
  pillow 92-3
horsetail 196
hyssop 85, 104, *108, 110*, 111,
  211

I

ice cubes 206
ices 46-51
indoor gardening 144-51
insect repellents 82-7

J

jasmine *99*, 211
  tea 62, 63
jelly, herb 76-7

L

lavender *51*, 78, *84*, 85, 87,
  104, 108, *124, 129, 130*, 172,
  183, 184, 186, 192, 211
  bottles 84-5
  bundle, dried 132-3
  essential oil 94
  foot cream 187
  growing 138, 140
  ice cream 52
  potpourri 107
  sachets 88, 91
  wreath 128
leaves: frosted 55
  herb potpourri 104-5
lemon balm *64, 142, 143*, 211
  lemonade 64
  tisane 63
lemon thyme *51, 170*, 215
  sorbet 50-1
lemon verbena *52, 77*, 104, 138,
  170, 179, 208
  & orange splash 178-9
lemonade, lemon balm 64

lime (linden blossom) *102*, 104, 215
  skin freshener 182-3
liqueurs 66-71
lovage 136

M
marigold 78, 104, *106*, 184, 186, 192, 209
  & apricot ice cream 49
  potpourri 106
marjoram 111, *114*, *152*, 159, 204, 212
  & poppy basket 121
  rosemary & thyme bundle 135
  see also golden marjoram
may blossom *see* hawthorn
mayonnaise 38
Mediterranean mixed pot 140
melissa *see* lemon balm
melon with mint & violet *22*, 30-1
meringues, violet 57
mesclun 30-1
mice 10, 82
mint *17*, *87*, 136, 204, 206, 207, 211
  cleanser 193
  eau de cologne mint *193*
  ginger mint 60
  melon with 30
  pineapple mint *142*
moisturizer 194-5
moths 82, 85, 87
mustard & dill sauce 40

N
nasturtium 78
nettle 196

O
oatmeal 170
  scrub 175
oil, bath 173
orange: dried 96
  moisturizer 194-5
  peel, dried 90
  splash 178-9
orangeflower water 178, *194*
orris root 87, 102

P
paints 150-1, 152, 159
pansy 79
parsley *29*, *40*, *144*, 204, 206, 207, 213
  curly-leaved *112*, *146-7*, 151
pasta salad, tricolor 26

pelargonium *see* geranium
pennyroyal 87, 212
peppermint *28*, 60, 82, 184, 212
peppers, bell: chutney 74-5
  salad 25
perfumes 176-83
pesto sauce 42
pillows 88, *90*
  hop-filled 92-3
pink 210
pomegranate pyramid 162
poppy *134*, 213
  & marjoram basket 121
  seeds 75, 206
posies 108-13, 162
pot-holder, hanging 146-7
potpourri 102-7, 204
potato & sorrel soup 18-9
pots 136-43, 150-1
preserves 72-9
preserving herbs 204-7
primrose 78
purée, herb 38, *39*

R
ribbon *127*
rose *46*, *71*, 85, 104, *114*, 124, 162, 172, *180*, 186, 192, 213
  ball, red 119
  brandy 71
  candied petals 207
  garland 126
  hand cream 186-7
  heart, pink 118-9
  ice cream 48
  layer cake 54
  perfume 180
  posy 113
  potpourri, red 105
  sheaf 134-5
  steam treatment 195
  tea 62
  wreath *11*, 127
  see also rosewater
rosemary *34*, *78*, 87, 104, 111, 124, 132, 138, *160-2*, 172, *176*, *183*, *187*, 196, 204, 213
  bundle 135
  focaccia 34
  foot cream 187
  rinse 201
rosewater 190
  & witch hazel toner 192

S
sachets 88, *90*, 204
  bath 174

insect-repellent 87
  lavender 91
sage 104, 108, 111, 112, 124, 132, *136*, 159, *187*, 204, 214
  foot cream 187
  growing 141, 143
  pineapple sage 104
  red sage tisane 63
  rinse 201
salad burnet 206
salads 22-31, 204
salting herbs 207
sandalwood 82
santolina 143, 214
sauces 40, 42
savory 104, 111
scones, cheese & thyme 37
scrub, bath 175
seeds, dried 206
shampoo 199
sheaves 130, 132
  cinnamon & rose 134-5
skin freshener 190
  lime 182-3
soap, pure 172
soapwort *196*, 198, 214
  & egg shampoo 199
sorbet, lemon thyme 50
sorrel *18*, *19*, 214
  & potato soup 18-9
  French sorrel *159*, 214
soups 14-21
southernwood 85, *87*, 108, 111, 208-9
spices 130, 160
  sweet powder 90
splash 178-9
steam treatment, rose 195
strawberry: & cheese salad 28
  plants *159*
sweet cicely 28
sweet powder 88, 90, 93
sweet woodruff 60, *65*, *172*, 210
  summer cup 65

T
tabbouleh salad 29
table settings 162
tansy *87*, 215
tarragon *44*, *69*, 204, 207, 209
  vinegar 78, *79*, 207
teas 60-3, 204
  rose petal 62
thyme 37, 78, *88*, 104, 111, 124, 136, *138*, *154*, *160*, *175*, 204, 215
  & cheese scones 37

essential oil 94
golden thyme 159
  in fruit box 154-5
  pot, with pebbles 138-9
  rosemary & marjoram bundle 135
silver thyme 108
see also lemon thyme
tisanes 63, 204
tomato chutney 74-5
toner 190, 192
tortilla chips 35
tree 116-7, 167
  Christmas, decorations 164
tubs *152*
tussie-mussies *see* posies
twig ring 129

V
vanilla 215
  & rose perfume 180
vine twig ring 128
vinegar, herb 78-9, 207
viola *57*, *157*
  basket 157
violet 78, 215
  candied 207
  melon with 30
  meringues 57
vodka 69, 178

W
walnut 211
  footbath 189
willow 196
window boxes 158-9
witch hazel 190
  toner 192
wood: outdoor containers 152-9
  scenters 100
  shaving mixture 96-7
woodruff *see* sweet woodruff
wreaths *11*, 72, 124-9
  lavender 128
  rose, on willow 127

Y
yarrow 196

Credits

Storey Communications, Inc. editor: Gwen W. Steege

Cover design by Jill Coote

Cover photographs by Di Lewis

Text and design production by Jill Coote

Photographs by Di Lewis and The Garden Picture Library pages 136-7 (Linda Burgess), 139 (John Glover), 140-1 (John Glover), 142-3 (John Glover), 154 top right (Lamontagne), 157 top right (Brian Carter), 158 (Jon Bouchier), 159 top right (John Glover), 202-3 (Marianne Majerus), 204-5 (Lamontagne), 205 (Mayer/Le Scanff), 206 (Mayer/Le Scanff), 206-7; Harry Smith Horticultural Photographic Collection pages 152, 156 right; herb portraits by Stonecastle Graphics Ltd.

Color illustrations by Nicola Gregory